W

Dreams

Working with
Dreams

*Understand your dreams and use
them for personal and creative
development*

RUTH BERRY

How To Books

Published by How To Books Ltd,
3 Newtec Place, Magdalen Road,
Oxford OX4 1RE. United Kingdom.
Tel: (01865) 793806. Fax: (01865) 248780.
email: info@howtobooks.co.uk
www.howtobooks.co.uk

First edition 1999

British Library Cataloguing in Publication Data
A catalogue record for this book is available from
the British Library

Illustrations by Jenny Lewin
Cartoons by Mike Flanagan
Cover design by Shireen Nathoo Design
Cover image PhotoDisc

Produced for How To Books by Deer Park Productions
Typeset by Euroset, Alresford, Hampshire
Printed and bound by The Cromwell Press, Trowbridge,
Wiltshire

NOTE: The material contained in this book is set out in good
faith for general guidance and no liability can be accepted
for loss or expense incurred as a result of relying in particular
circumstances on statements made in the book. Laws and
regulations are complex and liable to change, and readers should
check the current position with the relevant authorities before
making personal arrangements.

Contents

List of Illustrations

Preface

Most of us dream every night and yet we tend to forget our dreams when we wake up. We rarely stop to consider what our dreams mean, or how they could enrich our lives. Yet our dreams can help us to understand problems in our everyday living and to find a way forward when we don't know which direction to take. They can give us a new look at our intimate relationships and our emotional difficulties. They can also unlock our imagination and help us to become more creative.

In this book I will tell you how to remember some of your dreams and record them in a dream diary. You can then find out how to analyse your dreams, exploring the world of dream symbolism. You will begin to find out how your dreams act as a mirror, showing you hidden aspects of your true self and helping you to achieve healing and balance in your life.

Because your dreams have meanings that are unique to you, the book also shows you how to begin creating your own dream dictionary. You may eventually decide to form a dream group with some friends, working together to increase your dream power.

I would like to thank my daughter Jenny Lewin for providing the illustrations.

Ruth Berry

WORKING WITH DREAMS

How could I get a better night's sleep?

Why do I keep dreaming about falling?

Why am I stuck in a rut with my work?

What does the colour purple mean in my dream?

Why do I keep on dreaming about number 27?

Is my relationship over?

Why did I dream about earwigs last night?

Why do I feel depressed?

What is my true path in life – why am I here?

Is David the right man for me?

Should I move house, or stay put?

Why did I dream about living in a tumbledown cottage in the middle of a dark wood?

Do we dream in colour?

Why can I never remember my dreams?

Why do I dream that a man is chasing me with a knife?

Why are my dreams important?

If you are interested in your dreams, then this book is for you!

1
Learning About Dreams

LOOKING AT WHY WE DREAM

Theories about dreams

Although scientists are now fairly sure that we all have dreams, nobody has yet fully explained why we dream. If we are deliberately deprived of dreaming sleep, then we will catch up on dreams as soon as we can by dreaming more than usual. This suggests that dreams are necessary to us in some way. Various explanations have been put forward as to why we dream:

1. A dream is simply a sign that the sleeping brain is ticking over and interpreting signals coming in from the outside, such as the sound of a dripping tap. This theory hardly seems adequate to explain our more involved dreams.

2. Dreams are the brain's way of sorting out information from waking life. Useful information is then stored and the rest is forgotten. According to this theory, the brain will grapple with ideas and solve problems while we are asleep.

3. Dreams are a form of wish fulfilment process, where we can fantasise about what we cannot have, or do, in waking life.

It is probably true to say that we dream for all these reasons. Dreams do seem to help us to process information and also to explore our emotional needs. When we are asleep the **conscious brain** relaxes its control, so that we are able to sort out ideas and feelings that are normally pushed to the back of our mind.

The need for dreams

Some studies have shown that if people are deprived of dreams for a few days they tend to become irritable and find it hard to concentrate. People may even begin to have hallucinations. This suggests that dreams are certainly necessary for our mental and emotional health. Oddly, other studies have failed to show the same effects when people are not allowed to dream. Yet the original finding – that dreams are necessary and important – feels right instinctively. People have always been fascinated by their own dreams, and we tend to believe that they convey meaningful messages. It does not seem likely that they could simply be irrelevant by-products of the sleeping brain.

Forgetting our dreams

Although our dreams are important, we tend to forget most, if not all, of their content when we wake up. There are several reasons for this:

- The time factor. Our dreams take up approximately a quarter of our sleeping time. That is roughly two hours a night. If we were to remember them all, it would take up a great deal of our waking hours.

- We are normally too busy getting on with our waking life to bother thinking about our dreams. Introverted people, who spend more time analysing their thoughts, tend to recall more dreams than extroverts do.

- If the information processing theory about dreams is correct then it would be logical that we forget the content of dreams that our brain has labelled as useless information.

- We may also forget dreams that have a high emotional content, particularly if we are not comfortable with our inner feelings. Often, however, these are dreams that can be very valuable to us, pointing out where our conflicts lie.

EXPLORING SLEEP PATTERNS

Scientists have found out a lot about the electrical rhythms in the brain by wiring people up to electronic measuring devices. Our brain rhythm alters according to different states of consciousness. Each different type of brainwave is referred to by a different letter of the Greek alphabet:

- **Beta.** This is the normal rhythm of the brain while we are fully awake.

- **Alpha.** This is a slower rhythm, which appears when we are relaxed and drowsy, for example when we are listening to music, daydreaming, or relaxing in the bath.

- **Theta.** As we fall asleep the brain goes into this rhythm, which is even slower than alpha.

- **Delta.** This is the slowest rhythm of all and it appears when we are deeply asleep or anaesthetised. It can also appear in the deep meditation states achieved by yogis.

REM sleep

During sleep the brain also shows periods of activity connected with **rapid eye movements**, which are called **REM sleep**. Research has shown that many of our dreams occur during this phase of sleep. If you have had dogs, you will have noticed them twitching and maybe woofing faintly while they are in REM sleep, which suggests that they may be dreaming. Recent research suggests that we do dream during other sleep phases as well as during REM sleep.

REM sleep in humans begins about 90 minutes after we fall asleep. The brain waves speed up, heart rate and breathing increase, and blood pressure goes up. Although the brain is very active during REM sleep, the muscles are very relaxed – in fact the person may be almost unable to move. There may however be twitching, muttering, or even talking. The REM phase occurs in 90-minute cycles throughout the sleep period – usually four or five times during the course of a night. In between comes the deeper, calmer **non-REM sleep**.

FINDING OUT WHAT THE PSYCHOLOGISTS SAY

People have been fascinated by their dreams for thousands of years, and over the last century many psychologists have made a serious study of the subject. The pioneer in this field of research was Sigmund Freud.

Freud

Freud originally came from a medical background and he became interested in working with people who suffered from psychiatric problems. We need to bear this in mind when looking at his theories. Freud believed that dreams were manifestations of repressed desires, which were usually sexual in nature. These desires arose very early in childhood. According to Freud the mind heavily censors such ideas, and therefore much of the dream appears in symbolic form. The **symbols** were there to mask the true meaning of the dream. Modern psychologists do not tend to agree with this idea – the symbolic imagery is usually seen as the natural picture language of the sleeping brain.

Freud developed a technique of **free association**, which he used when interpreting dreams. The person simply followed a train of thought, beginning with a symbol that appeared in the dream. For example train – tunnel – entry – sex. This idea can occasionally be a useful one to use if one is stuck with a symbol which appears to make no sense.

Freud's work is very important because he was the first person really to try to gain some understanding of how the **subconscious** works. He believed that it affects our waking lives in important ways.

Jung

Jung's theory about dreams is rather different from Freud's. Freud tended to ascribe fixed meanings to a lot of dream symbols, whereas to Jung many symbols had meanings that were only relevant to the dreamer. He also broke away from the great emphasis on all dreams being about sex. Jung believed that our dreams were of great importance, and that we should meditate upon their meaning until they made sense to us. Jung found that many of his patients who were depressed or disturbed were not in touch with their subconscious. As a result of this, he claimed that we ignore the subconscious messages from dreams at our peril.

Jung often explored dreams that were part of a series, rather than simply looking at individual dreams. He was interested in the way a series of dreams would develop a theme which was important for the personal growth of the dreamer. He also developed the idea of **archetypes** – patterns of thinking which emerge from the collective psyche of all people. For example, people all over the world would understand the idea of motherhood – the mother is an example of an archetype. We will look at this idea in greater depth later on.

Hall

Hall worked to make dream analysis less mysterious and more available to ordinary people. Dreams were then no longer the province only of the experts. He believed that symbols appearing in dreams were directly expressed emotions and thoughts – they were not disguised so that the dreamer could not recognise them, as Freud had maintained.

Modern ideas

Therapists who work with dreams today usually encourage the person to find their own interpretation of their dream. Dreams are generally seen as a way of expressing suppressed hopes and feelings. The unconscious mind is bringing problems to the surface in order to help us to confront and resolve them. Symbolism in the dream is very important, and so is the emotional content. Usually dreams are seen as being relevant to the life of the dreamer at the present time, rather than harking back to childhood all the time.

THINKING IN SYMBOLS

Dreams are a product of our unconscious mind, which seems to think very much in symbols, rather than in language. So the dreams appear as pictures, which often build up into a kind of story. The symbols in a dream may mean very different things to different people.

Fromm

Fromm was another psychologist who was interested in dreams and he identified three types of dream symbols:

- **Accidental** symbols, which have a personal, individual meaning.

- **Conventional** symbols, which tend to have a similar meaning for many people. For example a car could represent a journey.

- **Universal** symbols, which have meaning common to all humans. For example the sun represents light and warmth.

A symbol that appears in your dream might fit into any of these categories. If you are stuck with what a symbol means to you, then it may be helpful to consider the more universal meanings. Try to begin taking note of symbols that appear in your dreams. Some of them may appear quite often, in which case they are important to you in some way. Symbols do not have to be objects. Colours, numbers, seasons, characters in your dream may all be symbolic in some way. For example perhaps you dream that it is autumn – is something coming to an end in your life?

Fig. 1. Common dream symbols.

Have a look at the dream symbols illustrated on page 16. See if you can think of a personal meaning, a common meaning and a universal meaning for each symbol. Some examples are shown in the table below.

Symbol	Personal meaning	Common meaning	Universal meaning
The sun	Summer holiday in Malta	Strength, leadership	Light, warmth, growth
A cat	My cat I had as a child	Feminine qualities, independent nature	Not known in all societies

If you begin to take notice of the symbols that surround you in everyday life, it will help a great deal when you begin to analyse your dreams. By thinking about symbols in this way you can begin to understand how a symbol may mean different things to different dreamers.

USING YOUR DREAMS

Every night our dreams can take us on a fascinating inner journey.

Listening to the subconscious

If we listen to these messages from our subconscious mind, dreams can help us in all sorts of ways:

- They can help us to identify areas of hidden conflict and worry which we have not confronted in waking life.

- They can work as signposts, which point out the best direction to take next on our life's journey.

- They can give us deeper insights into our personal relationships.

- Through dreams our bodies may sometimes warn us about potential health problems. They may also point us towards ways of helping those problems.

- Our dreams can help us to become more creative.

- Sometimes dreams can help us with problem-solving.

- Dreams may contain messages about other people and ways in which we could help them.

Conflicts

As an example, perhaps you dream of your boss as a pig, who gobbles up your lunch-time sandwiches. This dream could be telling you that you feel that your boss is rude and overbearing. We often suppress such knowledge for the sake of peace, but sometimes it is time to speak out.

Signposts

Dreams of this type often involve journeys and methods of transport. For example you dream that your car goes out of control and skids off the road. Perhaps the dream could mean that you have been overworking lately – cars often represent the self in a dream. Your dream may be telling you to slow down and take better control of your life.

Relationships

Perhaps you dream that your partner falls off a cliff. This could be wish fulfilment! Or maybe your relationship is not as good as you think it is – your subconscious might be warning you that you may lose your partner if you don't do something about it soon.

Health

Supposing you dream all your teeth are falling out. When did you last visit your dentist for a check up? Your subconscious may be giving you a gentle prompt.

Creativity

Simply working with your dreams and the symbols they present you with can help you to become more creative. Dreams have often acted as inspiration for writers and artists.

Problems

Sometimes we seem to gain fresh insight into a puzzling problem while we are asleep. A famous example is that of the research chemist who dreamed about a snake swallowing its own tail when he was trying to understand the structure of the benzene molecule. Benzene consists of six carbon atoms and six hydrogen atoms that link together in the form of a ring.

Helping others

If you suddenly dream that an old school friend is in trouble, try ringing him or her the next day. The subconscious mind is often sensitive to subtle messages that our waking minds may overlook.

QUESTIONS AND ANSWERS

What if I don't dream?

Psychologists now believe that we probably all dream. It is just that some of us find it hard to remember our dreams. As you read through the book you will find suggestions which may help you to recall some of your dreams.

Do we dream in colour?

There is a great deal of uncertainty and dispute about this. Many of us definitely do dream in colour. It seems odd that we should dream in black and white when our normal waking world is perceived in colour.

Is it safe to work with my dreams?

Our dreams can be very beneficial to us in developing self-awareness and creativity, so it is a pity not to take notice of them. Some people feel wary of delving into their subconscious, for fear of uncovering something unpleasant. However, writing our dreams down, working with them and talking about them often makes them less powerful and frightening. The process can be a very healing one, allowing us to let go of the past and live more fully in the present. Occasionally people may uncover something that they cannot deal with alone. If you should be really disturbed by any of your dreams, then you should seek professional help. Never feel afraid or ashamed to do this.

CASE STUDIES

Sarah
Sarah is 46 years old and married, with a daughter called Nicola who is 14. She worked as an assistant in a shoe shop before she had Nicola, but has never got round to going back to work. She would like to find a job that would give her more interest, but she doesn't know how to go about doing this. Her husband Mike works as a foreman at a local factory.

James
James is 37 and works with computers in an engineering company. He is rather bored with his work and feels that it does not really make full use of his abilities. He is single, having had several long-term relationships in the past, but has never been married. At the moment he

is not in a relationship, but he feels that he would like to settle down and have a family if only he could find the right woman.

Jo

Jo is 32 and married, with three children all under ten years old. The youngest has now started school and Jo has got a part-time job working as a nursery nurse in order to help make ends meet. She is always on the go and never seems to have any time to herself. She would like to be able to go back to college and gain some better qualifications. Her marriage is going through a very difficult patch and she feels that her husband Peter is becoming a couch potato.

CHECKLIST

1. If you are interested in finding out more about dream theories and research, then visit your local library. There is a bibliography of Further Reading at the end of the book.

2. Begin to notice how symbols occur in your dreams. Think about whether they have a meaning that is personal to you alone, or a more commonly understood meaning.

3. Think about what you would like to gain from studying your dreams. Try to identify particular problem areas in your life that you feel you could work with.

2
Preparing for Dreams

LEARNING TO RELAX

Making a bed-time ritual

You will have more success with dreamwork if you learn to relax fully before actually settling to sleep. A bed-time ritual is very helpful. Your own ritual will be a very individual one. Some of the following ideas may appeal to you.

- Keep to a fairly regular bed-time.

- Have a relaxing bath before bed.

- Wind down with a good book, a favourite TV programme, or a crossword puzzle.

- Have a warm drink.

- Share some special time with your partner if you have one.

- Follow an evening prayer routine appropriate to your religion.

- Listen to music, or to a relaxing tape. There are special tapes available to help you to relax – ask at your chemist, or health food shop.

No doubt you will be able to add other ideas of your own to this list. The important thing is to establish a routine that signals to your body that it is time to wind down and prepare for sleep.

Enjoying a relaxing bath

Bath-time can be a great way to unwind at the end of a busy or stressful day. Make sure the water is warm, but not too hot.

Using aromatherapy oils

Aromatherapy oils in the bath can help you to relax and also help to relieve aches and pains, which may keep you awake. Many ready mixed bath oils are available on the market. Experiment with these until you find one that suits you. You can also use pure essential oils, which are available from chemists and health food shops in small dropper bottles. These oils are very concentrated, so it is important to add no more than seven to eight drops to your bath water. For children no more than two drops should be added. Stir the water well to disperse the drops.

Essential oils act directly on your skin and also in the vapour, which you inhale from your bath. Take care with stronger oils such as mint and thyme – these may cause skin irritation. Check with your retailer, or a good book on aromatherapy, about recommended uses.

- **Lavender** is a very safe oil, helpful for tension, tiredness and depression. Put eight to ten drops in the bath.

- **Eucalyptus** is a good decongestant if you have a cold. It soothes muscular aches and pains. Put five drops in the bath.

- **Jasmine** is a good oil to use if you feel stressed or tired. It is uplifting for the spirits and also helps dry skin and PMT. Put eight drops in the bath.

- **Sandalwood** is sensual and relaxing, very good for insomnia. Put five drops in the bath.

Lighting colourful candles
Another relaxing idea is to bathe by candlelight. Choose a safe candleholder and place it somewhere where it cannot set light to curtains *etc*, in case you become drowsy. You can switch off the electric light if you wish, and lie back in the warm glow. Different coloured candles can be used to help you in different ways.

- Red – energising and stimulating.

- Orange – cheering and good for low self-esteem.

- Yellow – mentally stimulating and refreshing.

- Green – healing, relaxing and peaceful.

- Blue – calming and makes you feel serene.

- Purple – spiritually uplifting, good for meditating by.

- Pink – relaxing, soft and feminine.

- Black – imagine the black candle absorbing negativity.

- Gold or silver – for special occasions.

Bed-time drinks and snacks

It is not a good idea to have a heavy meal soon before going to bed. This can interfere with sleep patterns and cause indigestion. On the other hand if you are really hungry then that can keep you awake too. The answer is to have a snack such as a couple of plain biscuits. Milky drinks will help you to relax, but avoid tea and coffee last thing, because the caffeine in them may keep you awake.

Making herbal teas

There are various herbal teas available which will aid restful sleep and are available from supermarkets and health food shops, in teabags ready for use.

- **Camomile** is good for over-excitement and nervous stomach problems.

- **Valerian** is a potent tranquilliser and mild painkiller. It smells horrid, but there are teas available where valerian is mixed with other herbs.

- **Lemon balm** is refreshing, and a good restorative for the nervous system.

- **Hops** are good for insomnia, but they must be fresh ones. Put two teaspoons in a cup of boiling water and let it stand for five minutes to brew.

RECORDING YOUR DREAMS

Sleep studies show that we all have periods of REM sleep, which is the phase of sleep when many dreams occur. It therefore seems likely that we all dream, and yet some of us can never recall any dreams. Most people have had the frustrating experience of knowing that they have just had a dream, only to find it slipping away as soon as they are fully awake. Very often the dreams we do recall are those which are more vivid and meaningful to us in some way. However, it is possible to increase your dream recall considerably, even if you are one of those who are convinced that they never dream. The trick is to get through to your subconscious mind that you are interested in your dreams and wish to recall them.

Thinking positively

We tend to block our recall of dreams in various ways:

- By thinking that our dreams are meaningless or unimportant.

- By worrying that traumatic events from the past may return to haunt our dreams.

- By being too active and busy all day and not allowing time for reflection.

- For fear that we are not ready to be shown current events and relationships in their true light.

- For fear that we may have a nightmare, or somehow get too involved in our dreams.

These are all negative attitudes that we need to work through before we can be relaxed about dream recall. One good way to do this is by using positive **affirmations**.

Using affirmations
An affirmation is a positive statement about the way you want things to be. It is a gentle way of telling yourself that you feel in control,
When you are relaxed in bed, try one of the following affirmations just before settling to sleep. It will help you to concentrate upon your desire to recall your dreams.

- I allow myself to recall my dreams and explore their meanings.

- I am ready to listen to the wisdom in my dreams.

- I will remember dreams that are important to my life at the moment.

- I am relaxed and will remember my dreams easily.

You may prefer to make up your own affirmation. Experiment until you find one that is suitable for you.

Making a dream diary

Preparing your diary
Begin straight away to keep a notepad and pen, or a small tape recorder, beside your bed. Then you can record your dreams as soon as you wake up, before they escape. It will also act as another little reminder to your subconscious mind, saying 'I am ready to record my dreams'.

Buy a good A4 exercise book with a hard cover. This is to be your dream diary. If you want to you can personalise it by sticking interesting pictures on the cover. Use images that you find particularly interesting or dream-like. Soothing images such as soft white clouds in a blue sky, or a beautiful seascape would be good. Make your dream diary something special that you can treasure. Make it clear to friends and family that your dream diary is private unless you choose to share a dream. Otherwise you will feel inhibited about writing down some of your wilder and ruder dreams on paper!

Writing down your dreams
If you want to catch any dreams that you recall in the middle of the night then it may be a good idea to keep a torch by the bed. A few quick notes may remind you of your dream in the morning and the torch will save you putting the main light on. If you find that this disturbs you too much and prevents you from getting back to sleep, then it is probably best to record only the morning dreams. Try not to use an alarm to wake you up, because this can interfere with your dream recall.

Have a look at the sample page from Jo's dream diary in Figure 2 to see how to set out your pages. At the top of the page write the date and your location at the time of having the dream. Then write down your dream in as much detail as you can remember. Include everything, even if it does not feel like a 'real part' of the original dream. Even dream fragments can be important, so write those down too.

When you have written your dream down fully, put these headings underneath it:

- **Feelings.** Write down any emotions associated with your dream, such as fear, anger or frustration.

- **Colours.** Take note of any colours that seemed to have special significance, or which were out of place, for example red swans.

- **Theme.** Can you pick out a main theme in your dream? For example running away, or flying. Is it a recurring theme in your dreams?

- **Symbols.** Write down the main objects that appear in the dream. For example a car, a tree, a hen and so on.

- **Words.** Write down any words that seemed to be important in the dream.

- **Setting.** Where did your dream take place?

Date: 27.06.98   *Title:* Marshmallow dream   *Location:* Home

I was in a huge room like a school canteen. Three small boys were constructing something using bricks, toy cars and marshmallows. I ate a white marshmallow and then a pink one. The children had an aluminium mould for making more marshmallows. When nobody was looking I stole this and took it outside because it contained a yellow marshmallow that I wanted to eat. I felt very guilty. I was just finishing this marshmallow when the boys came out to look for the mould. One of them produced some yellow marshmallow stuff from behind my ear and stuffed it into my mouth.

Feelings: guilt and greed

Colour: pink, white and yellow (an odd colour for a marshmallow)

Theme: stealing something

Symbols: toys, sweets, mould

Words: none

Setting: school canteen

People; self, small boys

Other notes: body symbols: ear and mouth

Analysis: See later chapters

Fig. 2. A sample page from Jo's dream diary.

- **People.** Who were the main characters in your dream?

- **Other notes.** Make a note of anything else which seemed important, for example numbers, season of the year and so on.

Once you have done all this, make a final section for your analysis of the dream. Allow plenty of space for this, as you may find that you want to add more to it at a later date. We will look at dream analysis in more detail later on in the book. Use a fresh page for each new dream. When you have finished recording your dream, think of a suitable title for it, and put this at the top of the page. Then you can number the pages later on and make an index for your dream diary.

HELPING DREAM RECALL

There are various techniques you can use in order to help you recall more of your dreams. Once you have tried some of the ones described you will probably find that you can make new ideas of your own.

Making herbal sachets

We have already discussed the qualities of certain herbs when used in the form of herbal drinks or as oils in the bath. You can also use herbs to stuff a small scented sachet, which you can keep under your pillow. Make this sachet from a scrap of silk, wool or cotton and stuff it with any of the herbs which aid relaxation. You could also try some of the following:

- **Mugwort** has a smell which is reputed to aid dream recall and is also supposed to induce prophetic dreams.

- **Rose** has a familiar, relaxing and comforting smell. Like mugwort, it is reputed to bring prophetic dreams, particularly to do with love.

- **Rosemary** is supposed to be particularly useful in warding off nightmares and bringing restful sleep. It is a good herb to use if you are looking for the answer to a particular question.

Catching your dream before it slips away

When you wake up in the morning, try to remember your dreams before you move or stretch your limbs. Laboratory research on dreaming has shown that any movement can impair dream recall. Once you begin to move your active mind gets into gear too.

Talking about your dream
If you are able to share your dream with someone as soon as you wake up it often helps you to piece together the fragments. It will also stimulate you to remember parts that you would have otherwise forgotten.

Doodling
If you cannot recall any dreams at all, try doodling on a blank piece of paper. This can sometimes trigger a dream recall.

Observing your mood
Another useful trigger can be simply to observe what sort of mood you are in when you wake up. Sometimes the dream mood carries over for a few minutes after you awake.

Making a dream-catcher
This is a North American Indian idea. The **dream-catcher** is a net woven on a round frame and usually decorated with beads and feathers (see Figure 3). It is hung above the bed of the sleeper. The net catches the bad dreams, which then evaporate with the first rays of the morning sun. Good dreams drift down to the sleeper below.

It is satisfying to make your own dream-catcher. You can make the hoop easily from florists' wire covered with silk or raffia. Weave your net with silk and decorate your dream-catcher as you wish. Children love to have a dream-catcher above their bed.

INCUBATING DREAMS

Once you begin to get used to catching your dreams and recording them, you can begin to try incubating dreams. This means deliberately asking for a dream which will help you with a specific problem. For example:

- Why am I finding it difficult to stick to my diet?

- What can I do to improve my relationship with my sister?

- Why do I feel so tired at the moment?

You can also ask for a dream to clarify the meaning of a previous dream. For example:

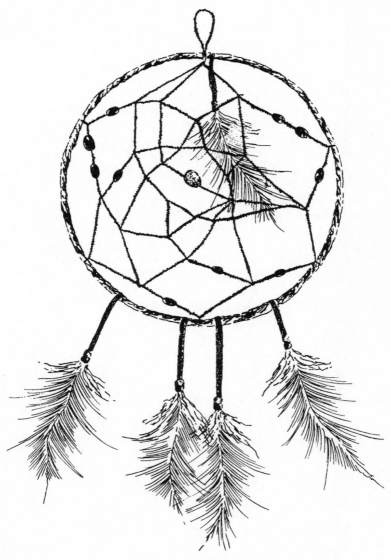

Fig. 3. A dream-catcher.

- What did my dream about the white horse mean?

- Why do I keep on dreaming about bags of rice?

In order to incubate a dream, concentrate on the question you have in mind before you fall asleep. One of the following methods may also help you to focus on your question.

Meeting your dream guide

This is a useful idea to use if you have a good visual imagination. When you are settled in bed, close your eyes and relax. Then imagine that you are climbing over a stile that takes you into a beautiful wood. Take time to explore your surroundings and enjoy all the things you see and hear. In this wood you will meet your **dream guide**. It may be a human being that you meet, or some kind of animal or bird.

Once you get to know your dream guide then you can call upon his or her assistance whenever you wish. Your guide will help you to remember your dreams and also to incubate dreams which are helpful to you. You may find your guide begins to appear in your dreams as well. If so, take special note of those dreams. Many North American Indian people used dream guides in this way.

Using a dream stone

Gemstones and crystals have been important to human beings for thousands of years. You can choose any stone which attracts you to use as your special aid. Keep it under your pillow when you go to sleep. Before you drift off, hold the stone in your hand and ask for its assistance. It is your positive intention which is at work here – without you the stone has no power of its own – but different stones do seem to encourage us to work with different energies:

- **Moonstone** can help with dreams connected with emotional problems.

- **Amethyst** is calming and balancing, useful if you suffer from nightmares or insomnia.

- **Quartz crystal** can help you with problem-solving. Think of the expression 'crystal clear' to remind you what this stone's special energy is.

- **Carnelian** is useful in connection with health and dietary problems.

● **Lapis lazuli** is a good stone to use for problems with children.

COPING WITH INSOMNIA

Insomnia can be a real nuisance, but try not to worry about it as this only makes matters worse. It can happen to most of us at times. Try reading for a while, or get up and make a soothing drink. If insomnia becomes more persistent, then consider the following points:

● Avoid high protein foods shortly before bed-time. These are hard for your stomach to digest and they may keep you awake or even give you nightmares.

● Are you under particular stress, or suffering from depression? If so, then seek professional help from a doctor or therapist if needs be.

● Check that there are not too many electrical appliances near your bed. You may be sensitive to the electromagnetic radiation from them.

● Avoid drinks containing caffeine, such as tea, coffee and cola. Their effects can linger for several hours.

● Occasionally insomnia may have another cause. If you are worried, see your doctor.

QUESTIONS AND ANSWERS

Would any kind of stone work as a dream stone?

Any stone which feels right to you is fine, but bear in mind they have different energies. You need to find one that is not too big to slip under your pillow. Some people find a special stone appears at the right time – perhaps on a walk by the sea, for example.

What if I still can't remember any of my dreams, even when I use the ideas described?

Don't give up! The more motivated you are to remember your dreams, the more likely you are to succeed. Research indicates that introspective people, who naturally focus more on their inner world, are more likely to recall their dreams easily.

What if I don't always have time to record my dreams?

Just relax. Above all dreamwork should be fun and interesting – a way of getting to know yourself better. If you miss a day or two, or even get fed up with the whole thing for longer periods, don't worry. Your dreams will always be there for you when you are ready to take an interest again.

CASE STUDIES

Sarah enjoys making her dream diary

Sarah finds that making her dream diary is fun and absorbing. She finds some postcards of animals and birds, which she had kept in a drawer since she was a teenager. She decides to decorate the cover of her dream diary with them. This makes the book feel special and she knows that it will help her to begin finding a way out of the rut that her life is in.

James begins to read more widely

James is interested to find out more about dream research and so he goes to his local library to look for books on the subject. He finds that as he becomes more interested in his dreams he begins to recall more of them. He then decides that it would be a good idea to begin his own dream diary in order to help him to understand his dreams. James finds that he often has frustrating dreams, where he is trying to get ready to go for an important interview and things keep going wrong, such as his shoes being too tight, or his tie the wrong colour.

Jo finds a little time for herself

Jo is worried about finding enough time first thing in the morning to write down her dreams, because the children are usually awake and demanding attention before she is fully awake. While shopping with her friend Alison, she spots a piece of clear quartz crystal three inches long and feels instantly drawn to it. She decides to buy it and use it as a dream crystal. She explains to the children about her crystal and tells them that when she is holding it in the mornings they must be very quiet. Before long they learn to respect her quiet time and Jo feels better for having a little time for herself.

ACTIVITIES

The activities sections throughout the book will help you to begin working with your dreams. You could also use them as part of a dream group (see Chapter 10).

1. Make a list of the benefits to your life that you hope will come from working with your dreams. This activity may highlight any particular areas of your life which you feel need attention.

2. Make a list of any difficulties you foresee, such as:
    _ what might prevent you from remembering your dreams?
    _ might there be any practical or emotional difficulties in writing your dreams down?

3. Begin to practise working with dreams by considering what James' frustrating dreams might be telling him.

CHECKLIST

1. Learn how to unwind properly and find out which relaxation methods help you the most.

2. Make yourself a dream diary and begin to get into the habit of using it.

3. Practise different ways of helping yourself to recall your dreams. Treat yourself to a dream stone, or make yourself a dream-catcher.

4   Try to recall all the dreams you can, even fragments. They can all give valuable insights.

5. When you get a bit more confident, try incubating a dream to help you with a particular problem.

3
Analysing Your Dream

RELATING DREAMS TO EVERYDAY LIFE

Now that you have begun to collect your dreams in your dream diary let's have a look at ways in which you can begin to interpret their meaning. The first and most obvious thing to do is to discover whether your dream relates in some way to your everyday waking life at the moment. Dreams often have aspects in them, or contain symbols, that relate directly to your current situation.

For example, perhaps you get a letter from your old school, asking you for a donation to support their appeal fund. That night you dream that you are back in the classroom, struggling with some difficult maths. Or perhaps you go round to a friend's house for coffee and her cat jumps upon your lap. That night you dream that a cat has sauntered in through your own back door and is helping herself to some cream.

Assessing the dream

There are two main things to look for if your dream seems directly related to your waking experiences.

1. The dream may simply refer to an event that happens to be foremost in your mind after your waking day. In this case perhaps your brain is just processing the information and either storing it away for future reference, or rejecting it as unimportant.

2. The dream may be working with a symbol that has cropped up in your waking life but is also important to you in some deeper way. For example, the school dream may be bringing up old feelings of insecurity that relate back to when you were bullied in the second form. In this case the dream is giving you an important message – this is an area of your life that you need to give attention to. The external event has triggered off a train of thoughts and feelings in your subconscious.

Have a good look at your dream and see how any of the following aspects of it may be directly related to events in your waking life now.

Location

Have you recently been to the location of your dream? Or perhaps you have seen it on television, or read about it in a book? What associations do you have with the place? How does it make you feel? Try to write down four words in your dream diary, which describe your dream location. For example, supposing you dream that you are on a warm, palm-fringed beach. Your four words could be 'sunshine, relax, peace and water'. The beach is evidently a pleasant place, where you would like to be. Perhaps you have recently watched a holiday advert on the television and your subconscious brain has stored this image away in order to remind you that you need a holiday soon.

People

Are you directly involved with any of the characters in your dream at the moment? Or have you seen them around somewhere? If not, then who do the characters remind you of? Again, try to write down four words to describe each character. For example, you dream about a woman in nurse's uniform. Perhaps your words are 'bossy, strict, caring, efficient'. Have you met anyone like this lately, or could the 'nurse' figure be an aspect of yourself?

Symbols

Have any of the objects in your dream appeared recently in your waking life? Why do you think they could be important to you? For example, you visit a museum and see some large Roman storage jars. That night you dream about storage jars with honey in them. Why have you chosen the symbol of a storage jar – what does it mean to you? In this dream you would also need to think about what honey means to you. Perhaps it could be a symbol of sweetness that you need to find in your life.

Feelings

How did you feel during your dream? Did your emotional state change during the course of the dream? Have you felt like this in real life recently? Very often if we are going through a period of emotional upheaval then we will have dreams that echo those feelings. These dreams are important, and often hold clues to helping us to sort out our problems.

Other aspects
You will discover for yourself other aspects of your dream that relate to
your waking life. For example, take note of colours, times, seasons and
so on.

Understanding your present situation
Your dream is like a mirror, showing you how you really think and feel.
To understand your dreams is to understand yourself better. A very good
way of beginning this process of understanding is to look at your
dreams and see ways in which they relate directly to your present
situation.

LOOKING AT EMOTIONS

Sometimes the way we *feel* during a dream is even more important than
the visual content of the dream. Read back through your dream and try
to imagine you are replaying the dream, like watching a film. How do
you feel during the dream? Was there one particular emotion, or did
your feelings change during the course of the dream? Write down
anything that comes into your mind at this stage, even if it seems silly
or totally unconnected to the original dream. Everything you write
down in your dream diary will be important to you. Listed below are
some key emotions to look out for in your dream:

● fear

● joy

● anger

● love

● embarrassment.

   How many more can you think of? Try to list some more and write
them down somewhere in the front of your dream diary, so that you can
refer to the list when you need to. As you collect more dreams you will
begin to notice that certain emotions come up time and time again.
These are the ones that you need to be dealing with and exploring in
your waking life. It may surprise you to find out which emotions are
appearing in your dream. If they are feelings that you did not expect to
find, then you should ask yourself if for some reason you are actually
suppressing them in waking life.

Feeling unusual emotions

Make special note of emotions that appear odd or out of place in some way, for example, hateful feelings towards someone whom you normally love. Try to look at these feelings honestly and objectively, and see if you can discover a hidden message there for yourself. For example, perhaps there is anger hidden away, which you dare not confront for fear of disturbing your comfortable existence?

Be careful not to over-react when exploring in this way. Sometimes inappropriate emotions in dreams do appear to be just that. Perhaps you have a passionate sex dream about your boss for example, whereas in waking life you genuinely don't feel that way. Our subconscious occasionally seems to develop a silly sense of humour, as if it were playing games with us, or trying out bizarre ideas just for a change. Or maybe the message that it is trying to put across is something rather different. In this instance the message might not be 'I am in love with my boss', but rather 'I need to lighten up a bit and take myself less seriously.'

DISCOVERING DREAM SYMBOLS

Another very important aspect of your dream is the symbolism that it contains. A symbol is something that is like, or represents, something else. For example a rose might represent peace and love. The subconscious brain tends to present ideas to us in symbolic form. Refer again to the notes that you have made under your dream in your diary. What particular symbols have you picked out?

Studying Jo's dream symbols

If you look again at the sample page from Jo's dream diary in Chapter 2, you will see that she selected 'toys, sweets and mould'. We will have a look at each of these symbols in turn.

Toys

Toys are generally associated with childhood. There may be a feeling of fun, being frivolous, 'toying with' an idea. Remember, however, that Jo has three small children and works as a nursery nurse. She wrote in her dream diary that toys were very much a part of her everyday life. She is constantly tripping over them, quite literally.

Sweets

The marshmallows in the dream are soft and fluffy, as well as good to eat. Jo associated them with spoiling herself and finding the sweet things in life. The colour is important here however, because some of them are yellow, rather than the usual pink or white. Yellow is the colour associated with an active mind, being well organised and communicating. Jo thought that this was very appropriate when she had just started her dream diary. She decided that writing down her dreams was beginning to help her to organise her thoughts. She thought that it was significant that she wanted to sneak away from the children to eat her marshmallows – her subconscious seemed to be telling her that she needed time alone, away from children.

Mould

Moulds are usually used for making lots of objects of the same shape. Jo felt that this could be to do with the repetitive nature of small children's play. She realised that she often feels stifled. She needs to get away – to go outside, as she did in her dream, away from the children and by herself. She is no longer fitting into the 'mould' of mother and carer. In fact part of her wants to 'break out of the mould'.

Finding your own symbols

After recording your dreams for a while, you will find that certain symbols crop up quite often. These symbols carry an important message for you. For example, supposing you often dream about blocked drains. What do you feel is blocked up in your life? It could be pent up emotions, or it could be a message about your physical body, telling you that you are blocking your energy in some way. Do you need to talk to somebody about your feelings, or do you need to go on a cleansing diet after a winter as a couch potato?

You will find that the symbols which crop up frequently will gradually change over a period of time, as your sleeping brain is mulling over fresh problems.

Recurring symbols

It is a curious fact that when symbols keep recurring in your dreams they have a tendency to crop up in real life as well, or else in books and films. Make a note of these coincidences in your dream diary. Maybe you dream about a falcon and the next day you see one flying alongside your car on the way to work. The falcon is sharp-eyed, swift and direct in flight. Does it have a message for you? Try this for yourself and see if you can discover dream symbols and waking symbols that overlap.

We will discuss dream symbols in greater depth in the next chapter. For the time being, just begin to be aware of the symbols that occur in your life and dreams. Consider how almost every aspect of your dream can be seen as a symbol in some way. Not only objects, but also colours, people, places and so on. For example, Jo could just have easily selected 'canteen, small boys, bricks', or 'cars'.

FINDING RECURRING THEMES

As you begin to build up your dream diary, you will find that certain themes or types of dreams tend to recur. These are showing you aspects of your world which are important to you at the moment. If a theme occurs over and over again, then it is quite likely that your subconscious is trying to get a message through to you, but you are not picking up the telephone, as it were. You are not listening to the message that is being put across, and so your subconscious is trying to put it across in slightly different forms, but following the same basic theme. Often these are themes that are to do with more deep-seated fears and anxieties, which sometimes, as Freud said, may hark back to when we were younger.

When we are children we acquire beliefs and attitudes which we carry forward into adult life. Sometimes your dreams are telling you that it is time now to have a good look at these beliefs, and perhaps discard ones which are no longer relevant or helpful in your life. For example, maybe you often dream that you are sitting an exam, or that you have failed horribly in an exam. If exams are not actually relevant to your life now, then perhaps you came from a family where it was desperately important to do well at school. Now that your subconscious has brought the subject up, you can begin to look at this belief in a more adult way, and perhaps begin to be easier on yourself.

Identifying your themes
We will look at some common dream themes in greater depth later on in the book. For the time being, have a look at this list of common themes and see if you can identify with them and perhaps add a few more of your own:

- falling dreams

- dreams where you are being chased

- dreams about water

- dreams about houses, which may or may not be houses you are familiar with

- travel and transport dreams

- dreams about delays and frustrations

- flying dreams.

When you begin to notice a recurring theme in your dream diary, you may find it helpful to add notes about what has been going on in your life. See if there is an emerging pattern that can be linked to the appearance of the dreams. For example, every time you go to visit your parents you might have dreams about water, in different forms. Sometimes it may be a raging flood, other times just a small trickling stream. Begin to build up an understanding about what these dreams are trying to tell you.

EXPLORING THE MESSAGE

There are many ways in which you can begin to unravel the messages hidden within your dreams. Try out all of the methods described below. You will gradually begin to find out which ones work best for you. Usually you will need to use a combination of different ideas before you begin to understand your dream. If you still find that you are stuck then put the dream on one side for a little while. The dream will still be there at the back of your mind and sometimes an event may occur that will give you a flash of insight and then you will say to yourself 'so that was what that dream meant'.

Using your symbols

Go through your dream and pick out any symbols that you feel to be important. Don't forget to include colours, numbers, seasons and even words, as well as objects and people. Now, looking at each symbol in turn, write down any ideas which spring to mind as to what you feel that symbol means to you. There are various methods you can use to help you.

Using a dream dictionary

These books can be very helpful in triggering off associations in your mind. However, it is important not to think that their interpretation will always be the right one for your own dream. Remember that symbols can mean different things to different people.

First record your dream

Write the dream down in as much detail as possible. Include everything, even if it seems stupid, or 'made up'.

Does the dream seem to relate directly to events in your waking life?

● Does it seem like just 'data processing'?

● Or does it seem to have a more symbolic content?

Now work on the symbols in your dream, using any of the following methods:

● a dream dictionary

● an ordinary dictionary

● myths and folklore

● explaining your dream to a friend

● drawing your dream

● free association.

Now leave your dream alone for a while

● You will learn more about your dreams as you read on in the book.

● Some dream meanings become clearer after a few days.

Fig. 4. Chart to help with dream analysis.

Using an ordinary dictionary
Simply look up the word for your symbol. The dictionary definition sometimes gives you a new angle.

Exploring myths and folklore
Some symbols have meanings that are often found in familiar stories. Think of a dragon for instance, who might be greedily sitting on his hoard of gold but isolating himself from companionship. Or the dragon might instead be a symbol of magical power. Dragons can be good or evil, depending upon the story.

Explaining your dream to someone
Simply describing your dream to a friend often helps you to grasp its meaning. As you put the dream into words that your friend can understand, you gain sudden fresh insight yourself. You might be describing a ring that appeared in your dream for example, and then you say to your friend 'come to think of it I had a ring very like that when I was about eight years old'.

Drawing your dream
It doesn't matter whether you think you are good at drawing or not. Seeing your dream as a picture will give fresh insights. You will probably find that you add extra bits to the picture as you go along, but this doesn't matter, because you are still communicating with your subconscious. Drawing can be a very valuable therapy in itself.

Free-associating
This is the method that was used by Freud. Just say any words that come into your head when you say the word for your symbol. See where the train of thought leads you. Try it now with these words, just for practice:

1. *Field*

2. *Elephant*

3. *Blanket.*

CASE STUDIES

Sarah dreams about horses

Sarah begins to notice that horses are appearing in her dreams. She has two dreams in which horses are galloping past her house. Then she dreams that she gets on the back of a black horse and rides it into the sea. When she thinks about horses she decides she feels they are powerful and beautiful animals. They are a way of getting to new places. Sarah feels that the message they are giving her is that she is ready to move on in her life, but not sure how to do so – sometimes the horses are just passing her by.

James is always being delayed

James continues to have frustrating dreams about trying to get ready for something and being constantly delayed. Usually it is an important meeting, or an interview, which he simply must get to. There are all sorts of trivial annoyances that hold him back every time. His car will not start. He finds that he is still wearing his pyjamas. He notices that his main feelings are of irritation and frustration. He decides that the dreams are related to his feelings about his real-life work.

Jo dreams about her hair going grey

When Jo wakes up one morning she is very relieved to find that her hair is its normal brown, and not grey after all. She has dreamed of looking in the mirror and seeing herself as looking haggard and grey. Jo decides that the dream is trying to tell her that she is not looking after herself. She is always taking care of others' needs before her own. She is afraid of getting old before her time.

ACTIVITIES

1. Practise your dream-work by considering the dreams in the case studies:
    –   What do you think Jo's dream might be telling her about her life?
    –   Why do you think she picked out those particular symbols?
    –   In view of his dream, what might James consider doing next in waking life?

2. Start an on-going dialogue, with both yourself and others, on symbols. When they appear in dreams and also in waking life, is this coincidence or is some other mechanism at work?

CHECKLIST

1. Make a note of ways in which your dreams relate to your everyday life.

2. Notice how your dreams can uncover deep-seated emotions.

3. Study symbols, not only in dreams; but also in the world around you.

4. Begin to notice the underlying themes that recur in your dreams.

4
Exploring Dream Symbolism

UNDERSTANDING ARCHETYPAL FIGURES

Although our dreams are personal messages to ourselves from our
subconscious, there is a lot of common ground in the type of images that
we experience. This shared **imagery** forms what Jung referred to as the
collective unconscious. Archetypes are the contents of the collective
image bank. So an archetype is a pattern of experience which is
common to all humans. It may appear in many ways, for example as a
symbol, an image, a pattern, a feeling, an idea, or as a person.

It is useful to be aware of archetypes, because they express ideas that
many other people can understand. So they can provide us with a kind
of structure, or 'mind map', drawing on the experience of others who
have been there before us. This can help to guide us towards finding out
what our dreams are saying. In this section we will look at some of the
most common archetypal figures which are likely to crop up in your
dreams.

Identifying archetypes
These are some of the archetypes that you might come across:

- male
- female
- child
- martyr
- fool
- stranger
- warrior
- priest
- priestess
- mother
- father
- victim
- nurse
- victor
- judge
- teacher
- monster
- bully
- saint
- hermit
- traveller
- baby
- boss
- savage

Have a good look through your dream diary and see whether you can pick out any characters that could be considered as archetypes. What do you feel those figures might be trying to tell you?

Very often an archetype appears as a representation of a part of ourselves, or of another person who is important to us in some way. If you have found some archetypes appearing in your dream, try to think who they remind you of:

● Are they like your partner in some way perhaps?

● Do they remind you of one of your parents?

● Or do you feel that the figure is mirroring some aspect of your own personality?

Sometimes both may be true – the archetypal figure is an aspect of yourself and also of another person.

The important thing is that archetypes are pointing out to you issues that you need to think about. Perhaps you need to be more like the figure you dream about. Or perhaps that figure is blocking your personal growth in some way. Very often the archetype is pointing out to you a role that you play in life.

An example

Jo had a dream about a wounded child, who lay on a bed all day and could not get up. She needed a full-time carer to look after her. Jo recognised this as a victim archetype, and began to realise that she often slipped into a martyred victim role, especially when she was tired after a long day. She realised that part of her would like to be the one who was being looked after.

Let's have a look at a few archetypal figures who may appear in your dreams.

Meeting the hermit

The hermit is a solitary figure, but not necessarily lonely. He or she often appears in our dreams when we are going through a period of spiritual growth. The hermit may indicate a need to withdraw for a while and spend time alone, apart from the hectic everyday world. The figure is telling you to listen to your inner voice – it has a message for you. Perhaps you are too quick to listen to the advice of others, and are ignoring your own instincts? The hermit may appear in any solitary form – as an actual hermit type, or as a wandering albatross, a monk or nun, or perhaps as the Lady of the Lake.

Meeting the warrior

The warrior is an assertive, aggressive character, who is very much in control. He or she is highly trained, efficient, proud and brave. How do you feel about this figure? Does it remind you of somebody that you know, or is it telling you that you need to stop being passive and stand up for your own rights? Do you feel that you would like to be the warrior, or is the figure opposed to you and threatening?

Meeting the monster

The monster is a common dream figure, especially dreaded by children. If one appears in your dreams, then confront it. Write down a really detailed description of it. How do you feel about it now? What aspects of your monster make it frightening? Monsters can be incredibly variable and personal beasts. They range from the grey, slimy Crawly Lump to the huge fire-breathing dragon. Remember that we all have monsters that we fear hidden away in dark corners. When your monster puts in an appearance, be glad – your subconscious is telling you that you are ready to face it and drag it out into the daylight.

Balancing male and female

Male archetypal energy is assertive and intentional. The female counterpart is passive and receptive. All of us have both energies within our psyche, but according to our sex and our upbringing, one tends to dominate the other. In the dream world we may experiment with different sex roles. This may apply to the physical body – for example a man dreams he has given birth, or a woman dreams she has a penis. We also try out different types of behaviour – for example, a quiet submissive woman dreams she is a Viking warrior, or a macho rugby-playing man turns into a geisha girl.

When we are going through a period of active change in our life rebalancing often needs to occur, so dreams of this sort will tend to arise. The psyche is saying 'this is what I need – forbidden or not!' Listen to its message. See if you can think of ways of integrating new balance into your life. For example the quiet woman could do an assertiveness training course, and the rugby player could take up growing roses.

FINDING THE ENERGY IN COLOURS

Not everybody is aware of dreaming in colour. For those of us who are, however, the colours can sometimes be very vivid and important. Now

Colour	Positive aspects	Negative aspects
Red	Energy, health, stimulation, sex, strength, excitement	Danger, violence, pain, frustration, anger.
Orange	Optimism, openness, health, renewal, warmth.	Arrogance, selfishness, superficiality.
Yellow	Creativity, clarity, imagination, intelligence.	Cowardice, fear, inhibition, anxiety.
Green	Growth, healing, money, grace, peace.	Avarice, envy, selfishness, loneliness.
Blue	Peace, serenity, wisdom, grace, spirituality.	Depression, introversion.
Indigo	Spiritual awakening, meditation, withdrawal.	Becoming too serious or detached.
Violet	Power, cleansing, spiritual and psychic awareness.	Tyranny, spiritual pride.
Black	Instinct, night-time, the subconscious, power.	Fear, depression, death.
White	Purity, cleansing, spirituality, perfection.	Spiritual pride, 'whitewashing'.
Brown	Grounding, nourishment, security, rest.	Dullness, depression, lack of inspiration.
Pink	Healing, love, femininity, gentleness, peace.	Helplessness, over-dependence.

Fig. 5. Interpreting dream colours.

and again a certain colour will seem to stand out, and is obviously trying to convey an important message. Each colour has particular energies associated with it and each of us also has individual associations with specific colours (see Figure 5).

Studies have shown that colours can definitely affect our mood. Pink, for example, is calming and healing, whereas orange is energising. If a colour appears prominently in a dream it may indicate that you need the energy of that particular colour at the moment, or that you are already opening up to changes in your life. Look out especially for colours that seem unusual or out of place, such as a red banana.

Finding your own colour associations

Make a list of colours and write down any associations that spring to mind as you think about each colour. This list will help you when colours appear in your dreams. Use some of the following ideas to help you.

Who wears this colour?

Does your brother always tend to wear blue? Or does the shy, retired schoolteacher next door always seem to wear brown?

Colour phrases

Think of any phrases you can, such as 'green with envy', 'red as a beetroot', 'the black night of the soul' or 'in the pink'.

Colour people

There are lots of these in myths and traditional sayings – for example 'lady in red', 'the white goddess' and 'the green man'.

Using your colours

If a colour seems to be sending you a meaningful message in a dream, then try using that colour more in your waking life for a while. Try some of the following ideas:

- Light a candle in your chosen colour and sit quietly for a while watching its flame.

- Wear something in your chosen colour.

- Sometimes colours are sending us a food message. For example if you dream of green, try eating more salad, or green vegetables.

- Buy something for your home that has your colour in it, or even redecorate a room with it.

NOTICING SEASONS AND WEATHER

Thinking about what the seasons mean

The seasons of the year have always been very important to human beings. Our ancestors, who lived much closer to the land, were of necessity more in touch with the rhythms of the year. Even in today's artificially controlled environment, the seasons are still deeply rooted in our psyche. As children we have known the joy of scrunching through autumn leaves, or lazing in long grass above our heads in the summer.

Your ideas about the seasons are naturally affected by the part of the world in which you have grown up, so they may differ from the ones described below. The important thing is to recognise that the psyche goes through cycles throughout our lives. These may be cycles of birth, death, growth, resting and so on. When the season is important in your dream, consider whether this reflects a cycle you are passing through at the moment, or need to embark upon.

Spring
Spring is usually seen as a time of rebirth, innocence, questioning and insight. It is connected to childhood in the human life cycle. Think of the phrase 'out with the old, in with the new'. Dreams involving spring tend to reflect new growth, new ideas, or taking a new direction in life. Perhaps you are thinking of embarking upon a new project, or conceiving a child.

Summer
Summer is associated with carefree days and easy living. It is the season of abundance, warmth and comfort. Things are going well. It is a time for holidays and parties – the season of sociable get-togethers. It relates to the time of youth, when we are full of energy, vigour and strength. Dreams where summer is prominent are telling you that the good times are here and projects will succeed.

Autumn
Autumn is about the completion of cycles, and reaping the reward for hard work that was begun earlier. It is a time of harvest, plenty, money and material goods. There is also the idea of storing up good things for future need, with the coming of winter. Dreams about autumn are telling us that we are nearing the end of a cycle. It is time to assess what we have learned, let go and move on. Autumn corresponds to mature adulthood, and feelings of responsibility and stability.

Winter
Winter is the fallow time, when we turn to contemplation. It is a time of death, rebirth, renewal and planting seeds. The energies are drawn into the self, for a period of hibernation. It marks the end of a cycle in life. Dreams about winter speak to us of inner awareness and spiritual growth. It corresponds to the season of old age, when the spirit is gradually released from everyday, earthly matters.

Expanding your ideas about the seasons

Drawing the seasons
Try drawing or painting a picture for each of the seasons. It doesn't matter if you don't think you are good at art. The important thing is to find out what your own associations are. What colours do you want to select for each season?

Celebrating the seasons
Make a list of the various celebrations throughout the year, such as Christmas, Easter, or festivals that occur in your own religion. Don't forget to include birthdays. Which is your favourite season? How do you feel when you think about that season? Do you have different feelings about other seasons?

Noticing the weather
Different weather conditions seem to come up quite frequently in dreams. They often reflect our emotional state.

Rain
Rain usually indicates a period of emotional cleansing. It washes away things that we have finished with, leaving us refreshed.

Snow
Snow is pure and white, giving a feeling of freshness. It may indicate a totally new start – a blank sheet.

Ice
Do you feel that something is frozen, at a standstill? Your emotions may be locked inside you, unable to flow. There is also the idea of 'skating on thin ice'.

Wind
Winds tend to blow things away and bring changes into our lives. A lot

Number	Positive meaning	Negative meaning
1.	New beginnings. Things which are about to happen. Independence and individuality. Determination. Inventions.	Wilfulness, selfishness, loneliness.
2.	Partnership in love or business. Balancing and co-operation. Agreement. Diplomacy.	Duality, being two-faced. Imbalance.
3.	Fun and parties. The trinity, or the triple goddess. Mind, body, spirit. Help, harmony and communication. Sharing, enjoyment, friendship and love.	Scattered energy, over-indulgence.
4.	Balance, stability. Four-square. Four-legged animals. Two couples. Team work, organisation, planning, making a solid foundation.	Dull, boring, and materialistic.
5.	Changes, expansion and travel. Moving on. The magical pentagram.	Misfortune, failure, loss. Problems and regrets.
6.	Harmony. Responsibility and maturity. Comfort, care, compassion, sharing.	Lack of compassion or responsibility. Disharmony.
7.	Inner wisdom and magical powers. Solitude, religious thinking and ritual. Great achievement through effort.	Fear and ignorance. Day-dreaming and escapism.
8.	Capability, success, attainment. Seeing things in their true light.	Strain, oppression. Inability to make the effort required.
9.	Fulfilment, wisdom, achievement. Self-reliance. Personal contentment and maturity.	Loss and having to let go. Loneliness.
10.	Completion and success. Satisfaction. End of cycle – a new one is beginning.	Oppression and weariness. Feeling stuck or martyred.

Fig. 6. Seeing traditional meanings in numbers.

depends upon the strength of the wind in your dream. A tornado or hurricane probably indicates that things are moving too fast, or getting beyond your control.

Storm
Storms are dangerous and threatening. You probably feel vulnerable at the moment, and your surroundings are unpredictable. Look for shelter until your storm has blown itself out.

Cloud and fog
Something is not clear to you at the moment, or perhaps a dark cloud has come into your life and covered up your sun.

Rainbow
This is a happy dream message, which signifies joy and celebrations. Rainbows often appear after a storm.

Sun
This is usually an indication of happiness, peace and inner strength.

Flood
Your emotions may be getting totally out of control. Do you feel overwhelmed by something? Or are you suppressing a flood of feeling? You will be able to add to these ideas for yourself. Take special note if the weather seems to change during your dream, for example, perhaps it gets colder or a mist comes down. Use these weather clues for hints about your true feelings about a situation.

COUNTING IN YOUR DREAMS

Sometimes a number seems to assume special significance in a dream. If you are lucky, perhaps it is a winning lottery number! Traditionally numbers do have special associations, so see if any of the ideas in Figure 6 seem to strike a chord.

Remember to look for your own number associations too, such as birthdays, your age, your house number, or perhaps a number that is lucky for you.

An example

James dreamed that he was taking a journey by boat along a river. He came to a place where there were two alternative ways to go, so he asked a passer-by for directions. He was told that he could carry on the way he was going, or else he could go 'through the seven locks, up the shining hill'. He decided that the seven locks symbolised something to which he had to find the keys. If he did this he could get 'up the shining hill' – this sounded more interesting than plodding on the way he was going. Seven is the magical number, but it involves work and effort too. He decided to do some studying at home, with a view to setting up his own business.

PLAYING WITH WORDS

Some people don't dream all that much in picture symbols. They tend to use words a lot and hear things being said to them in their dreams. A 'higher being' or mentor figure may come into a dream, to give us some profound words of wisdom. Words in dreams are sometimes puns, with a double hidden meaning. This type of symbolism may crop up more in your dreams if you have a particular interest in words. Perhaps your work involves words or languages. Or perhaps you are a keen crossword solver.

Quite often the words in a dream seem to carry a very profound meaning, and yet upon waking and writing them down, they seem trivial or meaningless. If this is the case, just go with it and leave the dream alone for a while. The meaning may become apparent in a few days. Sometimes the act of writing the dream down makes the double meaning become clear. It often helps too to tell your dream to somebody else, because as you speak the words aloud they reveal their meaning. For example, perhaps you dream about somebody called Mrs Owen – when you say the name aloud, you realise that in your dream this person 'owes' you some money.

The pun or meaningful phrase in your dream may actually be spoken aloud, or it may be presented in a visual form, even though it is a play on words. (See for example Sarah's wild boar dream below.) Dream puns can be very humorous. They are often liberating and cathartic, in the same way as humour is in waking life. Perhaps your pun may be telling you to lighten up a bit and not take yourself so seriously. Look at the funny side for a change. Let's have a look at the case studies now, for some examples of meaningful words and puns appearing in dreams.

CASE STUDIES

Sarah finds a wild boar in her airing cupboard

Sarah has a strange dream in which she goes to put some sheets away in the airing cupboard, only to find that a wild boar is asleep in there. When she writes the dream down, she begins to associate the animal with her husband. She realises that he has become a bit of a 'bore'. She realises too that his moods can be rather 'wild' and unpredictable. She needs to 'air' her feelings about all this.

James is not allowed through the doors of perception

James dreams that 'the doors of perception' are in his mother's kitchen. He is not allowed through them, because she says that he is not yet ready. They are secret, hidden by a grille, and James feels that something he needs to know lies beyond them. He feels frustrated and tantalised by this. He knows that his subconscious is almost ready to tell him something, but his waking self feels unprepared and not ready to cope with the revelation.

Jo meets a push-me-pull-you

Jo has a dream involving a strange beast, which she dimly remembers from a children's story. The beast is like a horse with a head at each end, and it is called a push-me-pull-you. Jo feels that the animal reflects the fact that she doesn't know herself whether she is coming or going, because she has so many demands upon her. She is pushed this way and pulled the other.

ACTIVITIES

1. Relate James' difficulty in going through 'the doors of perception' to your own life. Make a list of any techniques or ideas which might help you go through your own 'doors'.

2. Experiment with wearing different colours and notice how they make you feel. See your friends and other people in terms of specific colours and make a note of when these colours occur in your dreams.

3. Play 'Who am I' with friends. Decide which archetypal figure each of you is most like at the moment.

CHECKLIST

1. If an archetypal figure begins to appear in your dreams, take notice. Try to work out what this figure is telling you about your current situation.

2. Begin to be more aware of symbols of all kinds, not only in dreams but in your waking life as well.

3. Use colours to enrich your life and balance your energies.

4. When you record your dreams, look out for extra messages hidden in words and phrases, as well as in visual images.

5
Seeing Your Dream as a Mirror

SEEING YOURSELF AS DIFFERENT PEOPLE

One of the most powerful ways in which our dreams work is by acting as a kind of mirror. They show us aspects of ourselves that we are not always consciously aware of in waking life. Some dream theorists go so far as to maintain that all the characters who appear in our dreams are in fact different facets of our own personality. It is certainly true that things that we notice and find irritating in other people are often the very things which we wish to deny in our own personality. Freud called this process **projection**, because undesirable aspects of behaviour are projected outwards onto other people.

Dream characters may work in any of the following ways, or even in a combination of more than one of these ways:

- They may be telling us a few home truths about ourselves.

- They may be illustrating how we really feel about other people.

- They sometimes appear to point out aspects of our personality that we feel are lacking.

Acting the part of a dream character

A very good way to gain better understanding of a dream character is to try going into that character and acting out the role. This may take a bit of practice unless you are already an accomplished actor, but it can be great fun and is well worth working with.

Choose a character from one of your dreams. Now, simply pretend that you are that person, and begin to explain what you are doing in the dream. It helps to begin by explaining who you are. Say the words 'I am a grey monster', or ' I am a pirate with a wooden leg' or whoever you happen to be. Don't forget to think about how you feel, as well as what you are doing.

An example

Sarah dreamed that she was walking through a jungle and she met an explorer woman. The explorer was being criticised by a crowd of people, because she had been looking after a group of monkeys and had then left them behind 'on a high peak', overlooking the jungle.

'I am an explorer,' began Sarah, 'I have had to leave the monkeys behind. It was necessary because I needed to explore deeper into the jungle. They can take care of themselves now – they don't need me all the time. Anyway, they can still see me from where they are.'

What do you think Sarah's dream could mean? Who is the explorer woman? Remember that Sarah's daughter is 14 now, and Sarah is trying to work out what to do in the next phase of her life.

Changing roles

An interesting aspect of some dreams is that we actually change personalities half-way through the dream. Sometimes we are even aware of being two characters at once – the actor and the onlooker, for example. In waking life we sometimes say that we feel 'in two minds' about something. We say 'part of me wants to do this, and yet another part of me tells me that I should do that'. In dreams we can actually act out this feeling of duality.

We have seen that some characters in our dreams reflect aspects of ourselves, whereas others show us how we feel about other people. Obviously it is also possible for there to be an overlap, just as in real life we tend to choose to relate to people who are likely to help us in some way with our personal growth. Choose another of your dream characters now, and then try to answer the following questions:

● Who does this character remind me of?

● Could the character also reflect an aspect of my own personality?

● What lesson is the character trying to teach me about myself?

● Does the character have a message for me about a personal relationship?

Now, bearing these questions in mind, try acting as your chosen character, in the same way as you did in the previous exercise.

BECOMING EACH ASPECT OF YOUR DREAM

This exercise follows naturally from the last section, although it may seem a little odd when you first try it. What you do is to become each aspect of your dream in turn.

Mirroring yourself

The idea behind this is that not only the people, but in fact every part of your dream, can be a mirror of some aspect of yourself. The best way to explain how this works is to look at an actual example and see how it works.

James goes flying

James dreamed of a tiny yellow toy car that could fly through the air. Below it, on the ground, lots of huge diggers were tearing up the earth. The toy car was the only possible means of escape from the diggers. It narrowly missed their clashing jaws, and flew up through the clouds towards the sun.

James' immediate reaction was that the diggers represented the destruction of the earth. He felt great concern about the state of the environment and had recently joined Friends of the Earth. James tried going into the dream and becoming each aspect of it in turn:

- 'I am a tiny yellow toy car. I am like a toy car James had when he was a little boy. I am the only means of escape because I can fly above all the destruction and get an aerial view of what is happening. I am yellow because yellow is associated with the intellect. James must think of a way to stop the diggers.'

- 'I am a digger. I have cruel steel jaws and I am slowly tearing the whole world apart. There are lots of us, all over the surface of the earth. We are unstoppable and terrifying.'

- 'I am the sun. I am bright and give a message of hope. I warm and nourish the earth. If you can break through the clouds I am still here to help you.'

- 'I am clouds. I obscure your view. You must rise above me in order to find a solution to your problem.'

Try this method for yourself, using one of your own dreams. It is very powerful and will give you a lot more insight into your dream messages. Very often a symbol which has seemed obscure in its meaning will become clearer when you work with your dream in this way.

WORKING WITH EMOTIONS IN DREAMS

Meeting the shadow

The **shadow** is the part of the psyche that is hidden from us, where we store all the feelings and ideas that we don't really want to look at. Dream messages that have an emotional content are often telling us that it is time to have a look at that stuff.

The shadow may actually appear in human form in our dreams – often as a stranger, for example, or as a person like ourselves but perhaps with different coloured hair, or of the opposite sex.

James meets his shadow self

James dreamed that he was having a conversation with himself. The other self was standing on top of a little hill. The other self had dark hair, whereas James has light brown hair. James was about to go to a party with a group of friends, and was trying to persuade the other self to come too. The other self was being stuffy and pompous, and refusing to come down. After a while James got bored and wandered off.

It is easy enough to see that James was talking to a part of himself that he would rather not admit to. That part is pedantic and boring and doesn't have much fun in life.

Finding out what we really feel

Some dreams have quite a high emotional content and leave us feeling angry, guilty, afraid, sad or happy. The emotions that we experience in our dreams are not heavily guarded, as our emotions tend to be in waking life. This is why it can be so useful to examine dream feelings – because they are likely to give us an insight into how we really feel about other people and incidents in our lives. When we can be honest about our feelings then we can begin to break free of the bonds which normally hold us back. Such bonds are often formed through childhood conditioning and from fear left over from previous life experiences. They tend to clutter us up with a lot of heavy baggage.

Feeling guilty

Have another look back at Jo's marshmallow dream in Chapter 2. Here you will remember that Jo cast herself as the bad guy in the dream. She felt guilty about sneaking outside to eat some marshmallows. If bad characters appear in your dream who make you feel guilty, then imagine that you go back into the dream and talk to them. What would you like to say to them? Jo tried talking to her dream self in this way:

Jo:	Why do you feel guilty about going out to eat the marshmallows?
Dream Jo:	I ought to stay in and look after the children. Anyway, it's their marshmallow stuff.
Jo:	Why should you look after them all the time?
Dream Jo:	I'm responsible for them. It's my job.
Jo:	But you need time for yourself too. Why shouldn't you have sweet things in your life too now and again?

As a result of this conversation, Jo decided to go into town the next day with a female friend and treat them both to coffee. She felt a bit guilty for a while, but then she began to realise that she deserved it and really enjoyed herself.

If a dream makes you feel guilty it is quite likely that you are masking some hidden anger. There tends to be a veiled feeling of 'I want to do this, only you won't let me.' Find out who won't let you, and why they won't. In Jo's case it was really herself.

Feeling sad

Sometimes a dream can make us feel so sad that we even wake up in tears. This can actually be very cathartic – it often means that you are groping towards deeply suppressed feelings that you have been afraid to express. Again, have a good look at other characters involved in this dream. They are usually the keys to what is going on.

Feeling angry

Most of us have at some time had the experience of a jaw-clenching, tooth-grinding dream where we wake up tense and furiously angry. Find out who or what is making you feel this way, and talk it through or sort it out if you can. Blocked-in anger, like any suppressed emotion, can be very bad for you.

Sarah had a dream like this, where she dreamed that a bag of rice was jumping about all over her kitchen and laughing at her. She felt very angry towards it. The only association she could think of for rice was marriage, because you throw rice at newlyweds. She then began to realise that she was feeling angry and trapped in her marriage, but had not wanted to admit this for fear of rocking the boat.

EXPLORING DREAM HOUSES

Houses in dreams are often important mirrors of the way in which we see ourselves. If you dream about a house, write down a detailed description of it. It doesn't matter if you feel that you are making up

Fig. 7. A dream house.

some of your description – it will still come from your subconscious anyway.

Describing your house

- What type of house is it? (What sort of person do you see yourself as?)

- Is it big or small? (How do you feel in relation to other people?)

- Is your house cosy or chilly? Do you feel at home in it, or is it forbidding and unwelcoming? (Do you feel that you get on well with others, or do you see yourself as rather reserved?)

- Is the house old and rambling, or modern and compact? (Are you chic or do you feel better in tatty old clothes? How modern is your outlook?)

- Is it clean and tidy or is it chaotic or dirty? (What is your self-image like?)

- Does your house have any structural problems? (This can be an indication of a subconscious health warning, or an emotional problem.)

- Is the house well lit, or dim and dark? (This reflects your mood state – the house may be dim and dark if you feel depressed and well lit if you are cheerful.)

All these questions can give you surprising insights into the way that you view yourself at the moment. Perhaps the roof has blown off your house – are you feeling insecure and vulnerable at present? Or perhaps water is slowly rising up to flood your cellar – do you have deeply suppressed feelings that are threatening to engulf you? Perhaps your house is cosy and welcoming. Or perhaps it is too much that way, so that it is always full of other people? In this case, try to draw in your boundaries a bit and find more time for yourself.

Entering your house

Now let's have a look at different parts of your house and see what they can tell you about yourself.

- **The cellar** represents the darker parts of the psyche – the unconscious mind and the shadow self. Maybe you have something nasty and rotting down there – you need to get rid of that for a start!

Or perhaps your cellar is fill of vintage wine – have you been over-indulging a little bit lately? Have a look at what is down there. You will find that you have a pretty good idea what it means.

- **The attic** represents the mind and the higher, spiritual aspects of the psyche. Is yours full of clutter? Then it could be time for a good spring-cleaning session. Get rid of outmoded ways of thinking that are no longer useful to you.

- **The door** corresponds to your defence against the outside world. Is yours heavy and wooden, or is it partly made of glass? If it is all glass then you may feel rather vulnerable and transparent. On the other hand if it is too solid, then it might put other people off altogether. Does your door fulfil its purpose and protect your house, or can anybody just walk on in?

- **The stairs** show you the way up to your higher, spiritual self. Are they safe, or slippery? Can you get up them easily, or is there a problem of some sort?

- **The rooms** represent your everyday environment. Are they light and airy, or poky and dark? Do you feel happy in your house? How could you improve your house so that you feel more at home? Can you see ways of making some of these changes in your waking life?

- **The garden** also has to do with your environment. Does your house have a garden that you can relax in and unwind? If so, is there a fence around it or a hedge perhaps? Is your garden full of weeds, so that it makes you feel guilty? Or is it overly neat and orderly? If you are happy in your environment then you will probably feel at home in your dream garden and you will find it full of beautiful flowers, interesting nooks and crannies and secret hideaways. If you are really lucky, there might even be a gardener!

BEING WATER

If you dream about water, it can reflect your emotional state at the moment. For example, if you dream about a huge, calm lake, then your emotions are probably calm at the moment – you are going through a peaceful phase. Write down a detailed description of any water that you dream about. Then consider the following points and see how they could apply to your emotional frame of mind as well as to your dream water:

- What type of water is it – is it the sea, or a lake, pond, puddle, fountain, spring or flood?

- Is your water calm or rough?

- Is it deep or shallow?

- Is the water fast flowing or sluggish?

- Is it clear and sparkling, or murky, even polluted?

- What colour is the water?

- Is it dammed up in any way?

- Is the water cold or warm? Do you feel tempted to swim in it, or do you in fact fall in by mistake?

Use these clues in the same way as you did for the house exercise, in order to build up a picture of your current emotional state. Remember that it does not matter if you 'invent' some of your ideas. The more creative you are the better.

TRAVELLING IN DREAMS

Travelling and transport in dreams usually represent the way we view our way forward in life. Remember how James dreamed that his car would not start. What do you feel that this could mean?

Looking at types of transport

- **Cars** often represent the self or the physical body. What sort of car is your dream car? Is it a kind that you would choose to have in real life? Is it reliable, or is there something wrong with it?

- **Bicycles** can be a lot slower to get about on, and may be hard work, especially if the terrain is muddy or uneven. Perhaps your life is somewhat problematical at the moment?

- **Horses** are rather variable. They can be slow and plodding, or they can be fast, exhilarating power animals. A lot depends on the type of horse you encounter in your dream, and indeed, whether you actually like horses or not. This sort of difference underlines the pitfalls of having fixed meanings for dream symbols.

- **Travelling on foot** can be slow, but it is a good way of making sure that you have a good look at the terrain and that you don't miss things.

- **Flying** gives you a very good overview of your situation. Flying dreams are important enough to warrant a special section of their own later in the book.

Exploring the terrain
The terrain you travel over usually represents the way you view your life's path ahead of you.

- **Hills** get you to a higher place once you manage to get up them. They may represent tough obstacles, which are difficult to navigate. If you get up them easily then you are probably confident about tackling obstacles.

- **Barriers** such as gates or fences usually block your way forward. Can you find a way past your barrier?

- **Mud** or **swamps** are similar to water, in that they often represent emotional problems. They tend to be cloying or suffocating and hold you back. They can also make you filthy, so consider whether you have had an experience that has made you feel in some way polluted or violated.

- **Ravines** or **drops** make you feel insecure, afraid that you will fall down them and even be killed. You are probably feeling very uncertain about your future at the moment. Try to look for a safe bridge to cross over.

- **Crossroads** tend to appear when you have an important decision to make.

We often dream about travel or transport when we are subconsciously looking for a change in our lives. Often we are uncertain as to the right path to take, or the means of getting to where we want to be. Use your dream messages to help you to make the decisions and get you out of a stagnant situation.

QUESTIONS AND ANSWERS

I find it difficult to imagine myself as an inanimate object such as a kettle or a table. How can I get better at doing this?

It will get easier with practice. The secret is to not take the exercise too seriously. Try reading some children's books and poems.

What if I find one of my dream characters or objects frightening? Should I still try to act out the role?

There are no rules – don't do it if it feels too scary. But remember that it can be valuable to have a good look at the negative things as well as the positive. If a dream is really disturbing you, then ask for professional guidance.

Can I use symbols that crop up in real life in the same way as dream symbols?

Yes. The more you work with dream symbols, the more you will become aware of symbolic events in your waking life.

CASE STUDIES

James begins recycling

James thinks about his digger dream for a few days and he begins to realise that the diggers are in fact an aspect of himself as well as an external symbol. They represent his fear about global destruction, and he begins to understand that he is just as responsible for it as anybody else. As a result of the dream James resolves to do more to try and clean up his environment. He begins to take newspapers and bottles for recycling and to cycle to work whenever it is possible.

Sarah does some exploring

Sarah thinks about the explorer woman in her dream and she begins to see that she has actually reached a stage in her life when she is more free to 'explore'. She no longer needs to be at home all the time for her family, and in fact she is finding this rather stifling. She notices that animals are appearing quite often in her dreams and realises that as a young girl she always wanted to work with animals. She decides to visit the library and the job centre to see if there are any openings for her.

Jo does some spring-cleaning

Jo does the exercise visualising herself as a body of water. She sees herself as a pond. Children are paddling in her and she is full of children's toys. She has no outlet and her water is rather dull and murky. Jo decides to try to brighten her life up a little. She has a huge clear out and puts aside lots of toys that the children have finished with to go to a charity shop. She clears out her wardrobe too and buys herself a new dress.

ACTIVITIES

1. Make a list of all the characters who have appeared in one of your dreams. Against each name or description write down their characteristics. Then note down how these traits relate to any aspects of yourself.

2. Discuss with friends what type of house each person could be. Write down or draw your ideas first and then compare notes or images. Consider whether the way people see you is what you would expect.

3. Visualise yourself as a body of water. Go through the list of points for water dreams and in the light of this make notes of what changes you would like to make in your life.

CHECKLIST

1. Explore the ways in which different aspects of your dreams mirror parts of yourself.

2. Be aware of emotional issues that surface as a result of looking at your dreams.

3. Have a really good look round your dream house if one appears. If not, you could try visualising one and explore that instead.

4. If you are having travel or transport dreams then think about how you are 'moving' in your life. Perhaps you feel stuck, and ready for a change of some sort.

6
Using Your Dream for Healing

LOOKING AT BODY SYMBOLS

People often unconsciously use body symbols to express how they feel about something. Think of common phrases such as 'his heart was broken', 'you make me sick', or 'he's a complete air head'. Each part of the body tends to have its own associated ideas and emotions.

When specific body parts seem important in a dream they are often being used symbolically in this way. Your dream may be expressing a particular emotion – for example, we tend to link love with the heart, and anger with a clenched fist.

Alternatively the dream may be expressing an idea – for example, the feet are for going forward in life and the stomach could be for 'digesting' ideas.

Identifying body symbols

Have a look at the table in Figure 8, which suggests some of the common ideas associated with body parts. This is only a short list and you can begin to add your own ideas. Listen when people are speaking and hear how often they mention body symbols. Our body is a very important part of our life, and it is not surprising that this type of symbolism is so common. Look through your dream diary and see if you can pick out any body symbols. Below are a few common examples.

Finding your teeth falling out
This is a surprisingly common dream. It is sometimes just a natural anxiety – perhaps you need to go to the dentist! But teeth are for biting, so the dream may be about hidden anger. Or perhaps you feel that you have bitten off more than you can chew. Our teeth actually do fall out when we make the transition from child to adult, and again from maturity to old age. This dream therefore commonly occurs when you are at a transition point in your life.

Body part	Common associations	Examples of related phrases
Head	Thinking, intellect.	Using your head. Air head. Egg head. Keeping your head.
Heart	Love, emotions, compassion.	Broken heart. Heart of gold.
Arms/hands	Holding, grasping, carrying.	Having your hands full. Long arm of the law.
Legs/feet	Moving forward, staying grounded.	Feet firmly on the ground. Putting your best foot forward.
Tongue	Speech, gossip.	Sharp tongue. Evil tongue. Holding your tongue.
Eyes	Seeing the way forward, seeing things clearly.	Having your eyes opened. Sharp-eyed.
Ears	Hearing, listening.	A sympathetic ear. Walls have ears. Being all ears.
Nose	Being astute, or nosy.	Nosy parker. Having a nose for something.
Stomach	Digesting and assimilating.	No stomach for it. It makes me sick.
Lungs	Taking in energy or life.	Needing breathing space. Taking a deep breath.
Spine/neck	Support, flexibility, moral strength.	Pain in the neck. No backbone. Stiff-necked.
Mouth	Eating and communication.	Big mouth. Stiff upper lip.
Fingers/thumb	Picking up details, gesturing. Ring finger – marriage. Index finger – pointing	Pointing the finger. Putting two fingers up. Thumbs up/down. More sense in my little finger.
Shoulders	Carrying burdens and responsibilities.	Shouldering a burden. Having broad shoulders. Giving the cold shoulder.
Throat	Swallowing and speech.	It sticks in my throat. Swallowing a tall story.
Knees	Awe, fear, strong emotions.	On bended knee. Going weak at the knees.
Genitals	Sexuality, power.	Dick-head. Being a prick.

Fig. 8. Commonly occurring body symbols.

Losing your hair

Also common in dreams. It may mean that you are anxious about your health, or about ageing. If your hair changes colour in the dream, then you may be exploring new aspects of your personality. Our hair is a very important part of our appearance, so you may be exploring aspects of how you relate to others. Take note of the new hair colour and consider what it might mean.

Needing the loo

This often occurs in dreams as a gentle reminder that we had better wake up and go. If you dream this dream and find that you do not really need to go, then it is more likely that the dream is about something that you need or want to get rid of from your life.

BEING YOUR OWN DREAM DOCTOR

Sometimes people have a striking dream, or even a recurring one, about a particular area of the body. Studies have shown that this can occasionally be a subconscious health warning, so it may be worth taking note of. The message may be a simple one, telling you to cut down on junk food, or stop smoking. However, if the apparent message worries you, then it could be a good idea to tell your doctor. It does no harm to have a check-up, and your dream just might be a valuable early warning signal.

Remember that cars and houses sometimes represent the physical body, so if your car refuses to start, or if your drains are blocked, then this could be a health worry dream. Of course it would be wrong to imagine that you can diagnose your own illness, or treat it in some way. It is more a question of being aware of possible cues to slow down, rest more, eat less and so on. Dreams to watch for are:

- problems with your car
- problems with a house
- dreams involving violence or pain, *eg* being stabbed in the chest
- loss of hair or teeth
- dreams of premature ageing.

Any of these dreams could carry a health warning; or else they might be more about your emotional state. However, as mind and body are so closely linked, it is worth being aware of both aspects. A prolonged period of stress of any kind is often followed by illness in the physical body.

EATING FOOD IN DREAMS

Eating is one of our most regular waking activities, and also one of the most pleasurable. However, nowadays food is often also connected with guilt in a lot of people, wondering if they are eating too much food, too much fat, not enough cabbage and so on. If you dream about food, you need to consider different approaches to your dream interpretation.

Being nourished by food

Food is nourishment first and foremost. Therefore if you dream about food there may be a message about the way you nurture yourself.

- If you are looking for food, consider what is lacking in your life. Perhaps you are short of friends, or of intellectual stimulation – 'food for thought'. Or maybe the food you seek is of a more spiritual nature. Food is an obvious symbol for life itself, so are you enjoying life at the moment?

- If you are over-eating in your dream then you may be being over-stimulated in some way; or else a situation has become tedious and dull. Think about whether you are doing too much, or having too busy a social life. Or perhaps you are simply eating too much food in waking life and your subconscious is prompting you to cut down.

Looking at the colour of your food

Food colours in dreams may be unusual, or stand out in a striking way. This often means that you need more of the type of energy related to that colour. For example, if you dream about green foods, this can be your body telling you to eat more greens or salads. On a more spiritual level, the colour green is associated with healing and love. If you have recently been through an emotional trauma, then this could be the message in your dream. Try bringing the colour green into your life in one or more of the following ways:

- Eat more green foods.

- Light a green candle and meditate for a while by concentrating on its flame.

● Buy something green for your home.

● Soak in a green herbal bath.

● Buy yourself a green crystal such as aventurine or moss agate and carry it around with you for a while.

You can easily adapt this list for other food colours that may appear in your dreams.

Savouring your dream food
The quality of the food in your dream is very important.

● **Sweet food** can mean that you are enjoying sweet things in your life. If it is sickly or cloying, however, it could represent something you have had enough of, or something or somebody artificially 'sweet'.

● **Tough food** could represent a tough situation or character.

● **Bitter food** – what do you feel bitter about?

● **Savoury or spicy food** probably means that you are feeling satisfied and excited with your life at the moment.

● **Unsatisfactory or phantom food** – are you pursuing an unsatisfactory or illusory goal?

● **Nasty or sickening food** may indicate that whatever it is that preoccupies your mind at the moment is not really good for you.

Observing your surroundings as you eat
The place where you are eating, and possibly other people who are eating with you, can give other important clues. They will usually relate to the situation that your subconscious is trying to work with.

Thinking about eating food in dreams makes a useful transition between physical healing and more mental or spiritual healing. Food can bring a message on any or all three levels. The next two sections are about healing and balancing yourself more on the mental and spiritual levels.

RELATING TO ANIMAL SYMBOLS IN DREAMS

Throughout history humans have tended to regard animals as important messengers, both in waking life and in dreams. Shamans, who were the spiritual leaders in tribal society, often worked with animal symbols through trance, meditation and dreams. Each familiar animal or bird had its own associated characteristics and energies. Individual people, and sometimes whole tribes, often had a particular **totem** or **power animal**. This animal was the spiritual guide, mentor and protector.

If an animal or bird appears in your dream, then you can consider its message in several different ways:

- Does the animal remind you of an animal you have known personally, such as a pet or farm animal?

- Is it one of your favourite animals? (Children will often have a favourite animal, instinctively choosing one that will give them beneficial energies.)

- Does it link up with your birth sign, or another symbol in your life, such as a business logo or a car type?

- Does it feel as if your animal is giving you a special message? If so, then this could be your personal power animal.

Finding your power animal

A power animal is one that will give you energies or insights that you especially need. This can be a short-term thing for a period of life when you need a particular animal. It is also possible to find an animal that is a lifelong totem animal. This is an animal that feels especially important to you and will tend to appear in your dreams. Such an animal can be a guide and protector, helping to balance the energies in your psyche. Having pictures or other objects associated with your special animal can be very empowering.

Understanding animal energies

As with any symbol appearing in your dreams, it is important to realise that animals can carry a personal significance as well as a more widely recognised collective meaning. For example, somebody who has been bitten by a rabbit may not see the same cute cuddly animal that most of us would. Therefore some of the ideas below may not feel right for you, so go with your own instincts.

- **Cat.** Independence, female energy, mysterious, aloof, creature of the night.

- **Dog.** Loyal, trustworthy friend. Can be subservient.

- **Horse.** Swift, powerful, noble.

- **Pig.** Greedy, loves wallowing in mud. Intelligent.

- **Hen.** Fussy, mothering instinct, cosy.

- **Eagle.** High-flier, keen-eyed and far-seeing.

- **Owl.** Mysterious bird of the night. Silent, psychic and wise. Sometimes associated with death.

- **Fish.** Slippery customer, a cool water dweller. Some, *eg* salmon, are traditionally wise.

You will find more animals in the short Dream Directory at the end of the book. Try to build up associations of your own as well.

Imagining mythical beasts

Mythical animals can also have important roles to play in our dream world. You will find many ideas about them in myths and legends, which can also be a useful source of ideas about real animals.

- The **dragon** is a fire animal, which often appears guarding a pile of treasure, or fighting with a bold knight. There are many different types of dragons, but all are larger than life, fantastic and powerful. Chinese ones are often lucky.

- The **phoenix** is also associated with fire, and with reincarnation.

- **Mermaids** are interesting, as they are half human and half fish. There are mermen as well. Merpeople can be dangerous if they lure you beneath the waves, away from the mortal realm.

- **Fairies** can also be very dangerous and you have to keep on the right side of them. They may steal children, or human souls.

- **Unicorns** are mysterious, psychic, lunar beasts. They are rare and elusive and can only be captured by maidens.

TALKING WITH YOUR INNER CHILD

We all have an **inner child** – that part of our psyche that has remained with us since we were real children. When you feel in a light-hearted, silly or creative mood, that is when your inner child is showing itself. It may also manifest as a part of the self that feels small, defenceless or neglected.

The inner child quite often appears in our dreams and is a very important figure. If you dream about a child then consider:

- Is it a child you actually know, or have known?

- Or is it an unknown child that seems to reflect an aspect of your own psyche?

Remember that because your dreams often act like a mirror, your dream child may represent an aspect of yourself, even if it is a child you actually know in real life. Try to work out what it is about the child that reminds you of yourself.

Finding out how your inner child is feeling

Is the child in your dream happy and playful? Or is it angry or unhappy in some way? Some aspects of our emotional behaviour as adults are born in our early childhood, so it can be interesting to find out how your dream child feels. If your child is not happy, then try to imagine that you are talking to it. Find out what it wants or needs. Is there a way in which your adult self shares this need? If so, then could you think of ways of fulfilling the need? For example, perhaps your inner child is lonely – then you could try getting out more and making new friends, perhaps joining a group of some kind.

Seeing how your inner child is dressed

Is your child well dressed and cared for, or is it ragged, dirty and unloved? If your child seems to be neglected, then try to find little ways of pampering yourself more. Do something that you really enjoy, or buy yourself a new outfit or a little present. Nurture your inner child by caring properly for yourself.

Watching what your child is doing

- *If your child is playing happily* then you are quite likely going through a happy, creative phase in your life.

- *If your child is ill or wounded* then part of you may need healing. If you cannot do this for yourself then talk to a professional carer such as a priest or a therapist.

- *If your child is locked up or confined* then perhaps you need more freedom to express your playful, creative side. Try to have more fun and free time.

- *If your child is lost* then perhaps you fear losing part of yourself. Are other people dominating your life in some way, or are you overwhelmed by a difficult situation?

When you begin to look at your inner child dream, think about these and any other points that seem relevant. If you don't dream about a child, then you could try visualising your inner child, just as you may have done with the dream house and water exercises.

QUESTIONS AND ANSWERS

Is there a way to find my power animal even if I don't dream of one?

Yes. Your power animal may appear in waking life as an animal that you are especially drawn to. You can also try meeting your animal by relaxing and asking it to appear in a visualisation.

Can one have more than one power animal?

Yes – sometimes we need to work with the energies of more than one animal at a time. They may even appear to be conflicting ones, such as lion and deer. Each animal represents a different aspect of the psyche.

Are there other 'inner selves' apart from the child?

We all have many different inner selves, each of which is a kind of sub-personality of its own. Our different moods and behaviours can sometimes reflect this. You might meet an inner teenager for example, or a baby or a young adult. Conflicts that were unresolved at earlier stages of our lives sometimes appear in dreams of this sort. The beliefs and behaviours of people's 'sub-personalities' may conflict – which partly explains why people can be so unpredictable and contradictory.

CASE STUDIES

Sarah's inner child is ill

Sarah dreams about a child who is ill and lies in bed all day long. The child cannot play, or do anything for herself. When Sarah talks to her child, the child says that she longs to go outside and play with the others because she is bored, but her legs are too weak to stand on. Sarah realises that the dream is telling her that she needs to have more of a life outside her home and to 'stand on her own two feet'. She talks to the child and explains to her that she is well now and can stand on her legs perfectly well.

James meets a cat in his dreams

James dreams several nights in a row about a huge yellow cat that appears in different parts of his house and then on top of his computer at work. James feels that a cat is an independent creature – he remembers Kipling's story of the cat that 'walked by himself'. The cat is yellow, which is the colour associated with creativity and the intellect. James knows that the repetitive nature of his work at the engineering plant is stifling his creativity. He begins to wonder if he should go freelance. That way he could get a lot more variety in his work and use his brain more.

Jo joins a yoga class

Jo dreams that she is at the day nursery where she works. All the children are playing happily, apart from one little girl who sits in a corner crying. Jo feels very sorry for this little girl, and asks her what is wrong.

'I'm sick of all these children. I want my Mummy,' wails the child. Jo realises that she works with children all day long and then goes home to more of the same. She is totally neglecting her own inner child. All her dreams are telling her in different ways that she needs to nurture herself more. She decides do something about this and so she enrols in a yoga class one day a week and begins to have that evening for herself.

CHECKLIST

1. Be aware of body symbols in your dreams. They are important and can sometimes give a timely health warning.

2. Remember that dreams about food are about nourishing yourself. This may mean literally – by altering your diet – or it may mean nourishing your mind or spirit.

3. If an animal begins to appear from time to time in your dreams then it may be your power animal. Listen to the important message it has for you.

4. Get to know your inner child and take time to talk to it when it appears in your dreams. Find out ways in which you can see to its wants and needs.

7
Creating a Dream Dictionary

TAKING THE DRIVER'S SEAT

One of the most important aspects of learning how to work with your dreams is to realise that you, and you alone, are the expert on your own dreams. You are in control, in the driver's seat. So if you talk to somebody else about one of your dreams and they offer an explanation that does not feel quite right to you, you don't necessarily have to take their ideas on board. In fact sometimes talking a dream through in this way will put you in touch with your own 'gut feeling' about a dream, and so bring you closer to a true understanding.

It should be quite clear by now that dream symbols often have two distinct meanings. There is a common meaning, that most people would understand, plus a personal meaning, that is known only to yourself. This chapter is about how to build up a useful dream dictionary of your own, expanding ideas about your own personal symbolism. Before you begin, bear in mind the following points:

- You may feel that you want to keep your dream diary, and maybe even your dictionary, totally private. You might feel more willing to share your dreams at a later date when you are more confident.

- Keep your dream diary near your bed so that you can reach it easily. When you have written a dream down, take time really to 'listen' to the dream and get a feel for it, before you begin to analyse it.

- Don't be afraid of your own subconscious mind. It belongs to you and is a part of yourself that can offer valuable insights for personal growth.

- Encourage your subconscious to realise that you are now interested in your dreams. You can assist the process by bringing more creative activity into your waking life as well. Try painting, music, creative writing, dance, or simply being out in the fresh air more, or doing some gardening.

- Above all enjoy your dreams and the journey of getting to know yourself better.

We have already looked at some frequent dream themes, such as the house dream, water dream and travel dream. Before starting on your dream dictionary, let's have a look at a few more common dream themes.

LOOKING AT SOME COMMON DREAM THEMES

Falling
This dream can take many forms. Perhaps you fall off a cliff or down a deep, dark hole. Theories abound as to the cause of falling dreams. They are sometimes attributed to physical causes such as the simple muscle relaxation effect as you fall asleep, or even to bouts of indigestion! Symbolically, however, falling tends to feel dangerous and it could indicate that you feel out of control in some way. The context of the fall will give you more clues.

- **Falling off a cliff** often means that you are feeling very vulnerable, and unsure of the ground you are standing on.

- **Falling into a deep, dark hole** is often connected with a fear of exploring subconscious ideas.

- **Falling off a ladder**: think about whether you were climbing up, or down. Climbing up tends to indicate working towards a personal goal. Climbing down could mean coming down from a place where you felt unsafe, or it could be to do with climbing down into the depths of your subconscious.

Falling dreams often occur when you are going through a stage of rapid personal growth.

Flying
This is another common dream theme. You may find yourself flying high above the ground, enjoying a bird's eye view, or you may find that you can barely get off the ground. Flying dreams are often about your ambitions in life, so if you are soaring high then you are doing well. If

on the other hand it is hard work and you find lots of obstacles in your way, then perhaps it is time to reassess where you are going.

Another popular explanation for flying dreams is that they occur when the spirit enters the **astral body** and flies free. Obviously this interpretation depends upon your personal beliefs. It is certainly true that flying dreams are often associated with a sensation of great exhilaration and freedom.

Being watched

This dream can take many forms. You are sitting on the toilet and suddenly realise a crowd of people is staring at you. Or you find yourself stark naked in the middle of the supermarket. Such dreams usually involve embarrassment in one form or another. They usually indicate that you are feeling vulnerable or exposed in some way, and perhaps under attack from others. You might even have a secret that makes you feel guilty about something.

Wearing unusual clothing

Clothing tends to represent the attitudes and personality that we show to other people. If you are wearing ordinary comfortable clothes in your dream, then you are probably fairly comfortable with your current image. If, however, your clothes seem tight then it could indicate that you have 'outgrown' some of your attitudes or roles and need to 'change' them. If your clothes seem ridiculous then perhaps you are afraid of being laughed at, or maybe you just want to lighten up a bit and play the clown.

Sometimes you may find that you are dressed in the clothes of a particular character, such as Dennis the Menace. If this happens in your dream, then try to assess which aspects of that character you find empowering, or threatening. For example Dennis the Menace could be telling you that you need to be more carefree and childish, or even 'naughty'.

Being delayed or late

This type of dream has already been mentioned in James' case study. Everything goes wrong, you are late for an important appointment, or you miss the bus. Do you worry about being late in your waking life? Or do you feel that you are always in a rush, trying to fit too many things into your day? Perhaps you actually feel out of control of your life. If you feel that any of these things could be true, then you may need to relax more and 'chill out'. Try to spend time simply being, as well as doing.

Being paralysed

Perhaps you get stuck in a dream lift, or simply fall over and find that you cannot move. This kind of dream often occurs at times when we feel that life is frustrating. We feel unable, or unwilling, to make a necessary change. We might even feel 'paralysed' by fear. Is there a change that you know needs to happen in your life?

Some researchers have more physical explanations for the sensation of paralysis during sleep. During REM sleep, for example, the muscles are virtually paralysed.

DISCOVERING YOUR OWN SYMBOLS

By now you will probably be building up some ideas about dream symbols that have personal meanings for you. For example, perhaps you tend to associate bread with your mother, because she baked all the family's bread when you were a child. The more that you work with symbols, both in dreams and in waking life, the more insights you will gain.

Playing the symbol game

This game can be played on your own, or with a friend. It will help you to think in more intuitive ways about symbols and their meanings.

Look around and choose any object you see, just as you would for a game of I-spy. Supposing you choose the sun, for example:

- *What ideas do you immediately associate with your object? Be imaginative and think of as many ideas as you can.*
  Warmth, growth, holidays, sunburn, deserts ...

- *What feelings do you associate with your object?*
  Happy, relaxed, lazy...

- *Can you think of any stories, songs, films, etc connected with your object?*
  'The sun has got his hat on.'
  The sun god Apollo in Greek myths.

- *Do you have any interesting memories connected with your object?*
  Seeing the sun in partial eclipse when I was at school.

- *Try to describe your object to someone who doesn't know what it is.*
  It is our nearest star. It is very hot and warms the earth. It is bright, round and yellow ...

This game can lead you to all kinds of associations that you may not otherwise have thought of. It is very interesting to compare different people's ideas.

Looking for symbols in everyday life

Remember to keep an eye out for events and objects that could be symbolic in some way. For example we have all probably had the experience of a certain number which seems to crop up over and over again. It appears as a house number, a birthday, a lottery number and so on. Or perhaps your washing machine floods the kitchen - have you been feeling more emotional than usual? Looking for symbols in this way can be fascinating and sometimes highly amusing as well. It will certainly help you to understand dream symbols more readily.

MAKING YOUR DREAM DICTIONARY

You could begin your dream dictionary in the back of your dream diary, but it will probably get quite long after a while, so it is better to use a special notebook or file. The best thing to use is something that has an A to Z indexing system. An address book is one possibility, but even better would be a file with A to Z file dividers. That way you can add in more sheets of paper wherever you need them.

Divide each page up as shown in the example in Figure 9. The page shows an extract from James' dream dictionary. As you can see, some of the symbols he has chosen have already cropped up in his dreams, whereas others have been included simply out of interest. The dictionary will build up gradually as he goes along.

If you look at the entry under 'clothes', you will see that James has not yet put in any personal associations. Sometimes you will not think of any at first, so just go along with the common meanings until you find ideas that feel right for you. Use various sources to help you with ideas. Just to remind you of a few, you could use:

● a dictionary

● a dream dictionary

● myths and stories

● free association.

Looking again at James' sample page, you will see that some of his own associations are very personal. Look at the entry under

Symbol	Common meaning	Own meaning	Appearance in dream
Cabbage	Healthy green food. Dull person.	Yuk. I hate it. School dinners.	
Cactus	Prickly person, or difficult situation.	Auntie Mary's kitchen, because she has them on the windowsill.	
Cage	Fear, feeling trapped.	Hamsters.	
Clothes	Public image.		17th March, dream about being unable to find clean shirt for interview.
Computer	Logical thinking.	My work, creative ways of thinking.	11th April, dream about small boy playing on the computer.
Crossroads	Choice to be made. Unsure which way to go.	Ghost at crossroads near my house.	
Crowd	Strangers, anonymity.	Feeling alone in centre of London.	

Fig. 8. A sample page from James' dream dictionary.

'crossroads'. James has a particular association here with a local ghost, which means that crossroads could appear as being rather scary in his dreams! It is this kind of thing that makes your personal dream dictionary both useful and interesting.

FINDING SPECIAL SYMBOLS

Occasionally a symbol that seems to be particularly important may crop up in a dream. Sometimes this special symbol recurs in different dreams, or else it may come up only once but you just know that it feels important to you.

Special symbols may be well known ones that are found in myths and stories. They also appear as birth signs, business logos, religious symbols and so on. Or your symbol might be important to you alone. Either way, finding a special symbol in a dream can be very empowering and you should take special note when one occurs.

The special symbol may represent an aspect of your belief system or culture. More personal special symbols tend to represent an aspect of your own psyche. Look out for the following:

- **Religious symbols** – for example, the Christian cross.

- **National symbols** – for instance, the Welsh dragon.

- **Lucky symbols** – such as a four-leafed clover.

- **Mythical symbols** – like the Holy Grail in Arthurian legends.

- **Personal symbols** – such as an owl brooch you have had since childhood.

Deciding what a symbol means

If a special symbol does appear in your dreams, take time to decide what it means to you. How did you feel when you had the dream about the symbol? It can be very satisfying to work with special symbols in your waking life as well. Try any of the following ideas:

- Draw or paint your symbol and then put it somewhere where you will see it often, such as by your bed or in the kitchen.

- You might be lucky enough to find your symbol represented in an item of jewellery.

- Wearing your special symbol reminds you constantly of its meaning for you.

- See if you can find simple objects that represent your symbol. For example you might find it on a mug or a tea-towel.

- You might be able to adapt the symbol for your personal use – for example as a business logo, or as a letter heading.

CASE STUDIES

Sarah's T-shirt is too tight

Sarah dreams that she is wearing a sky blue T-shirt that is far too tight for her. It is particularly tight around her throat, and she begins to struggle, frantically trying to get it off but finding that she cannot. She wakes up in a state of panic and is very relieved to find that it is only a dream. When she writes the dream down she is not sure what it means, so she decides leave it alone for a few days.

Jo bathes in a fountain

Jo dreams that she is walking through a wood full of bluebells. She comes to a beautiful fountain of cool, blue-green water. She takes off all her clothes and sits in the fountain for a while. When she wakes up she feels very relaxed and refreshed, so she concludes that the fountain is a special symbol for her. Later that day she decides to paint her fountain. She borrows the children's paints and sits at the kitchen table. She hasn't done any painting for a long time and finds it very satisfying. When she has finished she puts her picture up in the kitchen.

James buys a sun sign

James has a strange dream about a big yellow sun sign. It has a smiling face, and makes him feel happy and full of energy. When he wakes up he feels that the sun sign is giving him a special message that he is going to have a really good day. He goes shopping later that morning and to his surprise sees a similar sun sign in a shop window. He buys it and hangs it in his living room. He finds that it gives him a very positive energy and begins to wonder if he could use it in a business logo.

ACTIVITIES

1. Practise your dream analysis on Sarah's dream in the case studies.
    – What do you think the dream might be about?
    – Can you think of a) a possible health meaning, b) a meaning to
      do with her personal life?

2. Start a discussion among friends about flying dreams. Take note of
    what people feel they mean and why they think flying is such a
    common dream. How do the theories connect to any flying dreams
    of your own?

3. Take time to relax deeply. Then ask for a special symbol for
    yourself to be shown to you.

CHECKLIST

1. Remember that you are the expert on your own dreams.

2. Look out for common themes occurring in your dreams.

3. Begin to create your own dream dictionary.

4. Be aware of special symbols in your dreams and try to use them in
    your waking life.

8
Understanding Some Common Dream Types

FACING NIGHTMARES

Most people will experience nightmares from time to time during their lives. A nightmare is a dream that leaves us with feelings of great anxiety, guilt, fear or even terror. They are quite common and some people have them frequently. The unpleasant emotions are often accompanied by physical symptoms – the person may wake up breathing hard, heart pounding, perhaps crying. Sometimes people will scream and wake others in the house.

Looking at the causes of nightmares

- Nightmares are sometimes caused by eating a large or rich meal shortly before sleeping. It is possible that the biochemical process of digesting the meal may interfere with normal sleep patterns.

- Withdrawal from alcohol, or other drugs such as some types of sleeping pills, may be accompanied by nightmares.

- Illness may also cause nightmares, especially if you are running a high temperature.

- Undergoing an upsetting experience during the day, or watching a disturbing film may cause nightmares.

- Paralysis nightmares, during which the victim feels unable to move, even if attempting to flee from danger, may be linked to the REM phase of sleep when the muscles are deeply relaxed.

- If you are going through a difficult phase emotionally, then it is more likely that you will experience nightmares. Worry and anxiety can interfere with sleep patterns, causing disjointed sleep, insomnia and nightmares.

Common types of nightmare

- Being pursued by something or somebody threatening.

- Feeling paralysed, unable to move or to escape.

- Exams, tests or interviews that go horribly wrong, or which one is totally incapable of coping with.

- Trying to get somewhere on time and being endlessly delayed and frustrated.

- Being strangled or suffocated.

- Experiencing or witnessing violence.

Nightmares are very personal experiences and you may well find that your own nightmare does not fit into any of these types. Sometimes the nightmare can be about something that nobody else would find frightening at all. The important thing is to acknowledge that you find your experience frightening and then try to deal with it.

Dealing with your nightmare

- First try to pinpoint what exactly it is that frightens you in your nightmare. For example, if there is a scary monster in your dream, then ask yourself what it is about the monster that really scares you. Is it the eyes perhaps, or its enormous size?

- Looking at your monster clinically in this way will begin to make it less frightening, even faintly ridiculous.

- Both modern therapists and more traditional dream workers tend to agree that the best way to deal with a nightmare is to face the fear head-on. If you start to have a recurring nightmare, then try to remind yourself before you sleep that this time you will face your attacker. You may then find yourself equipped with a weapon such as a sword next time your monster appears, or you may suddenly find a way out of your nightmare dilemma that you had not thought of before.

- You may find that you can talk to an attacker, if not during the nightmare itself then perhaps afterwards in a visualisation exercise. Try asking questions such as 'Who are you?' 'What do you want?' or 'What part of myself do you represent?' Write down any answers you get, even if they seem irrelevant at the time.

Fig. 10. A scary monster dream.

- Draw your nightmare. This is a very helpful method to use with children. They are good at inventing cages to confine their monster, or hoovering it up with a special vacuum cleaner.

- Talk about your horror with someone else. Try to find out what emotional experience it relates to.

- Appoint yourself a guardian. You could try taking a special crystal to bed, for example, that will protect you as you sleep. Children are often comforted by being told about their own special guardian angel.

- Remember to consider physical causes too, such as eating too late, or drug effects.

FINDING THE SECRET OF THE UNIVERSE – VISIONARY DREAMS

From time to time you may have a dream that feels especially important in some way. You may even feel, on awakening, that you have mastered the secret of the universe, or the meaning of life! Such dreams quite often prove disappointing on reflection, after you have written them down. What seemed like profound wisdom may turn out to be trite, unoriginal, or ridiculous.

However, many people do recall dreams that they feel have really changed the course of their lives. The dream may bring new understanding or help during a critical period of development. Such dreams are often recalled as rather mystical experiences and the dreamer may feel that the message has come from God, or from some other higher power outside the self. Literature is full of examples of this type of visionary dream.

Receiving help

The visionary dream may help us in different ways:

- It may lead to a new invention. The man who invented the sewing machine was guided by a visionary dream that gave him the idea of putting the hole at the tip of the needle.

- It may help us to figure out a problem. For example the chemist who worked on the structure of the benzene molecule finally got it worked out after dreaming about a snake swallowing its own tail. This image reflected the circular shape of the molecule.

- A visionary dream sometimes contains a warning or advice, either for ourselves or for another person. For example, Joseph's famous dream in the Bible, where an angel appeared and warned him to take his family away to safety in Egypt.

Characteristically the visionary dream seems to extend beyond the normal experience of the dreamer. Sometimes they may occur because our subconscious mind is busy working away on a problem while we sleep. At other times it really does feel as if we are receiving some sort of guidance. In either event, visionary dreams are often important and one should pay them special attention. Warning dreams in particular should be listened to.

TAKING HEED OF DREAM WARNINGS

Warnings in dreams are quite common and vary from everyday 'reminder' dreams to more important ones such as the health warnings discussed earlier.

Reminding yourself in dreams
Reminder dreams are small warning dreams that occur when our subconscious is prompting us to get on with everyday tasks that we have put off. For example you might dream about a cross man in an office labelled Inland Revenue. Have you forgotten to fill in your tax return form? Dream messages of this sort can be useful in drawing our attention to things that we know deep down ought to be done.

Warning dreams
Perhaps you dream that your washing machine floods the kitchen, only to find that it happens in reality the next day. This is probably because you have picked up on subtle cues such as the washing machine making a slightly unusual noise. This type of DIY dream often connects up with messages about the self as well as our home environment. The washing machine dream is connected with water – it may occur at a time when you are feeling extra emotional, tearful and upset. So if your household appliances begin to play up – either in your dreams or in real life – then have a look for symbolic messages of this kind. Ask yourself:

- What does my dream symbol represent? For example, supposing you dream that your drains are blocked up. Drains are for getting rid of unwanted stuff, especially of the liquid variety. The dream may be drawing your attention to a physical problem, such as constipation. Alternatively you may be holding on to emotional baggage that you would be better off without.

● What can I do to follow up the warning? Looking at the drain example, perhaps you could try to eat more roughage or drink plenty of water. Or if you feel that it relates more to your emotional self then try to find an outlet for your blocked up feelings. Talk to somebody, or work your feelings off in physical activity or in creative ways.

Disaster warnings

Occasionally people have a dream that seems to be a clear warning about a disaster such as an accident while travelling. If you do have a dream of this kind that really disturbs you, then it is probably as well to cancel your trip. Even if no disaster happens, you will save yourself a good deal of anxiety about the trip. Try to think about what aspect of your journey is frightening you. Sometimes disaster dreams are actually warnings that something is wrong with our health, or with an important relationship.

Warnings about others

Sometimes our dreams will give us subtle hints that all is not well in a personal relationship. Maybe on the surface everything appears to be fine, but the dream message from our subconscious tells us that deep down we are not being fooled. For example you might dream about fire breaking out in a cupboard inside your dream house. This dream suggests that you are hiding away angry feelings. If you go on suppressing them they may eventually do considerable damage. If you have a dream of this sort that you feel could be to do with a relationship, then try not to ignore it – try to work out what the message is about and then talk it through with the person concerned.

Sometimes we dream that harm of some kind comes to one of our loved ones. Dreams of this sort are common, so don't panic! First of all, consider whether the dream could actually be a warning about a problem such as a health issue. If not, then think about whether the person's problem is actually mirroring part of your own psyche. For example, you might dream about a lost child. This dream could really be about some aspect of your own inner child that you lost while you were growing up.

Exploring warning dreams

If you have a warning dream then you might like to explore some of the following questions:

- Is there some aspect of my life that I need to sort out?

- Have I been putting off something that 1 know needs to be done, such as going for a health check or getting the gutters mucked out?

- Am I suppressing looking more deeply at some aspect of a relationship, perhaps in order to keep things peaceful?

NOTICING COINCIDENCES IN DREAMS

Coincidences make a fascinating study, both in dream work and in waking life. If you study your dreams regularly, you may find dream themes that coincidentally link up with events in waking life. For example, James dreamed about a 'little deer' that was running around his living room and trying to get up the stairs. He especially noticed that the deer had long, protruding tusk-like teeth, which struck him as rather odd. The next day he visited a museum with his young niece and to his surprise he saw a specimen of the same deer in a glass case. It was a Chinese water deer. This was a clear case of a coincidence, because the two events were apparently unrelated, and James had no idea why he had had the dream.

Keeping a coincidence diary

Coincidences of this sort in our dream world are rather mysterious, and much more common than you would think. You might find it interesting to keep a special coincidence diary, collecting instances from both waking and dreaming experiences. If you do this, try to set a few ground rules as to what you count as a coincidence. For example:

- Set a deadline of say 24 or 48 hours. Your two experiences must be no further apart than this.

- To count as a coincidence the events involved must not have an obvious causal connection. For example it would not count if you read the same thing in two books that were about similar subjects.

- The dream part of the coincidence must come before the waking life part.

- A dream coincidence must link up with either a waking experience, or with somebody else's dream. The same thing happening in two of your own dreams does not count.

Attuning to coincidences

When you begin to record coincidences they will seem to appear a lot more frequently in your life. This could perhaps be simply because you are tuned into them and noticing them. If you experience dream coincidences, then study the related symbols and events carefully. Look out for key words, puns; and prominent characters. Ask yourself:

- What could this coincidence mean?

- Why is this message appearing in different ways in my life?

- If a person or animal figures in the coincidence, try to decide if it could reflect an aspect of yourself.

- Does your coincidence prove to be meaningful, or is it more of a random one? Both types of coincidences are interesting to record and study.

- Can you explain your coincidence? If so it is not really a true coincidence.

  Remember that the events in a coincidence must be apparently unrelated in what has caused them.

EXPLORING OTHER TYPES OF DREAMS

We have already had a look at some of the more common dream themes in Chapter 7. Here is a further selection of dream types that you may come across.

Dreaming lucidly

A **lucid dream** is one where you become aware that you are dreaming. With practice it is possible to manipulate one's dreams and make events go the way you want them to. As mentioned earlier, this can be very useful for dealing with nightmares. The art of lucid dreaming is quite complex however, and whole books have been written about it. If you become interested in the subject have a look in your library or bookshop to see what is available for further study.

Forecasting the future

Precognitive dreams – those where we seem to predict future events – are quite common. They may take the form of a warning or coincidence. James' dream about the little deer is one example. The incidents involved may be of great importance, but more often they seem to be random and trivial.

Sarah dreamed that somebody handed her a coin with a man's head on it, and some foreign writing that she decided was Greek. The next day she went to the bank, and the lady in front of her in the queue handed a coin to the cashier. She explained that she had been given the coin in some change, but it was a foreign one. The lady did not know where the coin was from, but the cashier looked at it and said that it was Greek.

This is a typical precognitive dream – it feels meaningful and interesting and yet it seems to be pointless. Nobody really knows why or how such dreams occur, but many people who keep dream diaries soon find that they are cropping up regularly. Like coincidences, they seem to occur more often when you begin to show an interest in them. In fact you could argue that all coincidence dreams are also precognitive to some extent.

Dreaming of death

It can be very frightening to dream of your own death, or the death of a loved one or a well-known person. It can occasionally come as a health warning, or as a precognitive dream. More often, however, the death involved is not a physical one. It is more of a psychological death, to do with the death of old belief systems or ways of behaving. Therefore the death dream can be very empowering, bringing a feeling of much needed release.

It is important to remember that death can be seen as a beginning of a new life, as well as the ending of the old. It is often a case of 'out with the old, in with the new'. The change that is coming into your life may feel difficult and frightening, but it is most likely ultimately for your own good. We tend to resist the change through fear of the unknown and clinging on to the familiar. If you dream of death ask yourself:

- What feared change does your dream represent?

- Is there an aspect of your life that you know needs to change?

- Are you in fact about to embark on a new job, a move, a new relationship, or other major change?

- Are you worried about your health, or that of a friend or loved one?

Recurring dreams

Recurring dreams are especially important because they show that the inner self is trying repeatedly to get a message across. The conscious mind is probably not really responding to the message. Sometimes exactly the same dream happens over and over again, and sometimes the content varies a bit but the theme is always similar. If you have a recurring dream, or a recurring dream theme, then try to explore it by asking questions such as:

- What message is this dream trying to convey?

- Why am I reluctant to hear that message?

- Is the dream about a hidden fear that I would rather not bring out into the open?

- Is it about some hidden aspect of a relationship that I fear to admit?

- Is it about a neglected talent that I know I should make use of?

Wish fulfilment dreams

Earlier we discussed the fact that one of the functions of dreaming seems to be wish fulfilment. The type of dream where your secret desires come true can be fun and liberating, but on the other hand it tends to leave you with a vague feeling of disappointment when you awake.

If you find that you are often experiencing this type of dream, then it is fairly obvious that your waking life is not as fulfilling as you would like it to be. Try to pinpoint the areas of life that are not satisfying to you, and then set about finding ways of improving the situation. For example, supposing you have a recurring dream about being king of a vast empire. This would suggest that in waking life the opposite is true and you tend to feel insignificant and powerless. There could be many ways of improving this feeling – perhaps a change of job would help, or even a new creative hobby. Try to get in touch with your real needs.

Sexual dreams

Sexual dreams are a natural part of the dream world and tend to appear regularly. Studies have shown that creative people tend to have more of them – possibly because freedom of expression generally is linked with freedom of expression sexually. The important thing is not to feel guilty about your sexual dreams, even if you find yourself enjoying a good time with somebody who is totally unavailable in real life!

Remember that the sexual urge is a normal aspect of living in a physical body.

Surprisingly it is quite common to dream about having sex with somebody that you don't fancy at all in waking life. People also sometimes find that they have rather surprising sexual dreams involving animals and so on. In this case it is important to remember that each aspect of your dream can be thought of as reflecting an aspect of yourself. So if you dream you are making love to a horse, for example, then think about what aspects of 'horse' you feel are energising and exciting. Remember that the dreaming mind is not restricted by moral censorship. When you have a sexual dream then notice:

- Who are you with?

- Is this person an appropriate real-life partner or not?

- Do you actually fancy this person in waking life?

- What is the setting of the dream? Is it a safe private place, or is it somewhere public or dangerous in some way? If you feel exposed then you are probably experiencing some sexual anxiety at the moment. If you are in a house, then consider what messages the house gives – for example, a Victorian setting might suggest repression. Places like hotels and airports suggest a transitory, impersonal feeling.

- If you have a bizarre sexual dream, such as making love with an animal, or (if you are usually heterosexual) with someone of the same sex, then take note of how you feel. Do you feel disgusted and embarrassed, or is the dream exciting and liberating? Remember these dreams may link up with your creative and energetic urges.

- Is your sex dream a wish fulfilment dream?

QUESTIONS AND ANSWERS

What if I have a recurring dream that I cannot fathom out?

Try discussing it with a friend. This often opens up your ideas. Alternatively, just before dropping off to sleep try asking yourself for another dream that will clarify the problem. When you wake up write down all the dreams you can remember, even fragments, and see if you can connect any of them with the original dream. The connections may not be apparent straight away.

What if I feel that my sexual dream is odd, or disturbing?

There are therapists who are trained to help if you really feel that you have a problem. Don't be afraid to seek help and reassurance.

Supposing I have a warning dream involving another person. Should I tell them about it or not?

This is a tricky one. It partly depends on how well you know the person – you don't want to get labelled as a complete crank! You should also consider whether the person is someone who is easily upset. If so, then it could be counterproductive to get them into a nervous state, which might prove totally unnecessary. On the other hand, if you know the person well and you feel that the warning could be relevant, then perhaps you might tell them about your dream. Stress that it was just a dream, and leave it up to them to decide whether or not to take action.

CASE STUDIES

James dreams about a whirlwind
James dreams that a whirlwind comes rushing towards his house and then straight through the ground floor. He is watching this from upstairs, and although he can feel the house shaking he is unharmed and the house remains standing. James decides that perhaps this is a warning dream about a forthcoming event that will shake him up. He wonders if it could be about the possible changes with his work situation.

Sarah meets a tall flobbery monster
Sarah is walking alone down a dark lane in her dream, when to her horror she sees a 'tall flobbery monster' blocking her path. She becomes semi-lucid in this dream and remembers that it is a good idea to confront her monster. To her surprise she discovers that the monster is friendly and he is sick of people running away from him. He is very lonely and glad to talk to Sarah.

Jo dreams that Lucy falls down a tower
Jo dreams that she is in a castle tower with her youngest daughter Lucy. Lucy is swinging about on the roof of the stairs. Suddenly she loses her grip and falls. Jo knows that she has fallen to her death and feels an agonising sense of loss. When she records the dream Jo feels very upset and frightened by it. But when she thinks it through she realises that she

feels she has recently 'lost' Lucy when she started school. The dream also reflects the fear she felt when she started school herself.

ACTIVITIES

1. Write down as many ideas as you can for coping with a recurring nightmare.

2. Start a discussion with friends about:
   - Whether it is possible to foresee future events in dreams.
   - How warning dreams arise and whether they come from within ourselves or via external forces.

CHECKLIST

1. If you suffer from nightmares, don't ignore them. Try to find out their cause and work with them.

2. You may find it interesting to begin a study of the coincidences that occur in your life.

3. Take heed of any personal warning dreams that you have. They usually occur for positive reasons.

4. If you dream of death don't be too frightened. Remember the dream may symbolise your fears about an important change in your life.

9
Expanding Your Dreams

LEARNING SIMPLE VISUALISATION TECHNIQUES

You can work with your dreams in greater depth if you learn how to do simple visualisation techniques. We have already begun look at these earlier in the book when, for example, you wrote about your dream house. During this exercise you were encouraged to be inventive and write down all your ideas, even if they did not actually seem to be a part of your dream. A creative visualisation is very like a dream, only you do it when you are actually awake.

Getting properly relaxed
It is important to be well relaxed before trying out a visualisation exercise. You may have your own favourite method of getting relaxed. Have another look at the ideas in Chapter 2. If you find it hard to get properly relaxed, then try going through the following stages:

● Find a comfortable position, either sitting or lying down.

● For the next few minutes just concentrate on your breathing. Don't try to alter it at all, simply observe the process. If your attention wanders, keep bringing it gently back to your breathing. After a while your breathing will probably begin to slow down as you start to relax.

● Starting with your toes and working slowly upwards, scan each part of your body for tension. If you find tense muscles, then take a deep breath in and really tighten them up. Hold the tension for a few seconds. Then on the out-breath, consciously release the tension and let go. Visualise all the tension leaving your body and soaking away into the ground.

● You should now feel much more relaxed and ready to begin your visualisation.

Exploring a garden

The following visualisation is a good one to try first. You need to get a friend to read it to you while you relax, or you may prefer to read it aloud yourself onto a tape before you start. Make sure that you don't rush the reading, and leave spaces whenever you see dots like this ... When you are more used to doing visualisations you will probably find it possible just to read them through beforehand and then go straight into them without needing to use the spoken words.

The visualisation

You are standing at the gate of a walled garden. Have a good look at the wall and then study the gate... when you feel ready, open the gate and go inside the garden. All around you are beautiful flowers and trees. Stand still for a moment and enjoy the rich colours and scents of the garden... Now you notice a little pathway going further into the garden, so you begin to walk slowly along it. There are lavender bushes on either side of the path and bees are buzzing peacefully amongst the purple blossom. Listen to their summer sound, and smell the wonderful scent from the lavender...

After a while you come to a bed of roses. What colour are they? You bend down and cup one of them in your hand and inhale its scent deeply. Linger for a little while to enjoy the rose bed... Now you walk on and you come to a fruit tree laden with one of your favourite fruits. Why not pick one of the fruits and enjoy its taste...

When you are ready, walk on again until you come to a seat in the sunshine, partly shaded by a tree. Sit here for a while and relax in your garden. What do you see? Perhaps there are birds among the leaves of the tree. Fluffy white clouds sail across a blue sky... What do you hear? A bird sings in the branches above your head and the leaves rustle in the breeze... What do you feel? The sun is warm on your skin and you feel the cooling breeze...

You are now free to explore your garden for as long as you wish. It is your own secret place and you can return here whenever you want to. When you are ready, follow the path back to the gate. Don't forget to close the gate when you come back out of your garden...

Being creative with visualisation

You may find it rather difficult to manage visualisations at first. Some people are naturally good at it and already use visualisations in their daydreams. Others do not tend to think in such a visual way. If you are one of these people, try visualising a familiar scene first. Imagine that you are standing in your own living room, for example. Look around you and notice as much as you can. Then gradually go on to visualise slightly less familiar surroundings, such as your local supermarket. Then try inventing a location – try imagining yourself on a tropical island, or at a fun fair. After that try being on the seashore, or deep in a forest. The possibilities are endless – just be creative and have fun.

Creative visualisation represents an interesting state of mind that seems to be half way between dreaming and being fully conscious. The mind is given free rein and allowed to be wonderfully creative, and yet we remain conscious and in control.

RE-ENTERING YOUR DREAM

Once you get good at creative visualisation, you can use the technique to re-enter a dream. In other words, you can replay a dream sequence by visualisation, and then alter the dream if you wish, or bring it to a satisfactory ending. This is especially useful for certain types of dreams.

Confronting fear
You can re-enter a nightmare and confront your fear. During a visualisation you can be much more in control of the situation, so you can change the dream until it no longer disturbs you.

Working on recurring dreams
If you have a persistent recurring dream, you can go back into the dream and try to find out what it is really about. Ask yourself 'Why am I here again?' 'What is this dream telling me?' You may find that you get a new angle on the dream. Perhaps a new character appears, or the story takes a slightly different course. Remember that you are in control and can make the visualisation progress in whichever way feels best.

Re-working a dream
If you have had a dream that you feel has an unsatisfactory outcome, then you can re-enter the dream in order to finish it in a way that feels satisfying. For example, in Chapter 3 Jo dreamed about her hair going grey. She could re-enter this dream and see herself with her hair its normal colour again, and her face radiant and healthy. This would help to remove the negative self-image that has been suggested by the dream. She could even imagine herself with a new hairstyle, or with interesting highlights in her hair.

Re-entering a dream gives you a chance to introduce new characters, or change existing ones. You can also change the story line or alter the script in any way you wish. It is rather like being your own film director, and it can be both fun and illuminating. It is a good idea to record the dream re-entry in your dream diary in the same way as you would an ordinary dream.

ASKING FOR INSTANT SYMBOLS

Asking yourself for an instant symbol is like doing a mini visualisation. The method can be used for help with any type of problem, as well as for gaining more insight into a dream message.

Finding a symbol

The message is simple – you just ask your question and then close your eyes and ask for a symbol that will help you to arrive at an answer. The trick is to catch the first symbol that pops into your mind, even if it seems an odd choice at first. The symbol must arise totally spontaneously, before your conscious brain has a chance to step in, so catch that first image, however fleeting it is. Try to describe this symbol to yourself, or to a friend. Go into as much detail as possible.

An example
Sarah felt that she was putting on weight and yet she felt unable to stick to a diet, so she wondered what to do about it. She asked herself for an instant symbol. The symbol that arrived first was a spade. Sarah described her symbol like this: 'I can see a spade. It is for digging in the earth. I am outside in the garden digging. I need more fresh air and exercise. The spade is for digging deeper.'

She decided that this meant she should 'dig deeper' into her own psyche, so she asked for a second instant symbol. This time she saw a clear, sparkling waterfall. Sarah remembered having read that one ought to drink plenty of water in order to avoid retaining fluid. She began to drink more water and to her surprise she lost several pounds straight away.

This example shows how one can work with instant symbols in order to gain insight into problems from the waking world.

Working on difficult dreams

You can work on obscure dreams in the same way. Simply ask for a symbol that will give you further insight into what your dream is trying to say. Remember that the process of describing your instant symbol is

very important. You can use the instant symbol method to help with
many of life's choices and problems, such as:

- Why am I stuck in this situation again?

- What is the best path for me to take?

- What is blocking my progress?

- How is this person affecting me?

PROTECTING YOURSELF IN YOUR DREAM

Using the creative visualisation method, it is possible to create special
weapons or guardians that you can call upon in the dream state.
Sometimes we wake up in the middle of a nightmare in a state of fear.
If this happens to you then it can be helpful to grasp your weapon or call
upon your guardian before drifting back to sleep again. You may even
find that they appear spontaneously in a dream once you are used to
them. The type of weapon or guardian you choose is entirely up to you
– whatever makes you feel safe is right for you.

Choosing a protector or weapon

Your dream protector or weapon will be something that makes you feel
safe and empowered. You might already know what it is – if not then
you can use the instant symbol method to find out. Simply relax and
then close your eyes and ask to be shown the best way of protecting
yourself in dreams. You can use your protector or weapon for defence,
warding off enemies and healing. It could be one of the following, or
you may wish to explore your own ideas:

- A **special crystal**. You may already have a crystal that you can
  imagine taking with you into the dream world. If not you can invent
  one.

- A **weapon** such as a sword, a laser gun or a small dagger.

- An **amulet**. This can be any small symbolic object that you can
  wear about your body. People have made themselves amulets for
  many thousands of years, often dedicating them for protective
  purposes with special magical powers. Sometimes amulets are of
  animal or human form, in which case you may find that they 'come
  alive' and work as a guardian as well.

- A **special light**. This might be a lantern, or even just a candle. It will illuminate your dark places and make you feel safe. This can be very helpful if you were afraid of the dark as a child. In fact many adults are still secretly afraid of the dark too, so if you are one of them don't forget to create a dream lantern.

- You might also like to imagine a special suit of **armour** that you can put on to protect yourself. An alternative is a protective **bubble,** or a **force field** that you can generate at will.

Meeting your guardian

The guardian is a dream figure who will protect and guide you. You can choose any form of guardian that appeals to you. If you do not already have a guardian then try doing a visualisation exercise and ask to be taken to a place where you will meet your guardian. You could start off in the dream garden or anywhere that feels right to you. The guardian can take any number of forms.

- The **angel** is a common form of guardian. People feel that they have great spiritual powers and can perceive a much wider view of things than humans can.

- **Animal guardians** may be very varied. Perhaps you will choose a fierce strong lion, or a swift, far-seeing hawk.

- Your guardian may be a **human being**, such as a knight in shining armour, or a wise old hermit.

- There are many **mythical beings** who make good guardians too. You could choose a mysterious unicorn or a fire-breathing dragon for example.

Your guardian may talk to you about problems that arise in your dream work. He or she may also give you gifts, or special powers that will help you during your dream journeying. A guardian may also guide you to your correct path in life, or introduce you to a special task that you must accomplish.

Once you have met your guardian he or she may appear from time to time in your dreams. You can also ask your guardian to help you with a dream re-entry session. If you feel tense or upset before you go to sleep then ask your guardian for help and don't forget about any special protector or weapon that you can use as well.

FINDING YOUR PLACE OF PEACE

Once you become familiar with the method of creative visualisation, you can try choosing a special place of peace that you can visit at any time. This can be any place that makes you feel peaceful and safe. It could be a wonderful garden, a place by the sea, a crystal cave, or a wood full of beautiful trees. It is entirely up to you – just use your imagination and create a place that is right for you.

Begin by relaxing and concentrating on your breathing. Then close your eyes and ask to be taken to your special place of peace. Imagine that you are walking along and you come to a flight of steps. There are 20 of them in all, going downwards. As you go down them, count down from one to 20 slowly. You will then find yourself in your special place. Use all your senses to imagine this place as fully as possible. This is your own private place, where nobody else can go.

When you want to become fully awake again, walk back up the 20 steps and count up from 20 to one. Open your eyes and stretch your body gently until you feel awake.

Using your place of peace

You can visit your place of peace whenever you feel stressed. It is a good idea to go there just before you go to sleep. It is also a good place to meet your guardian when you want help with a problem. You will probably find that you add bits to it gradually as time goes on and you think of more ideas. The main thing is to enjoy your special place and feel really at home there.

QUESTIONS AND ANSWERS

What if I find an unexpected guest or strange beast in my place of peace?

Ask them what brings them there and whether they have a special message for you. Remember that you are in control – this is your place. If necessary, evict them!

I find it difficult to do visualisations because I keep getting distracted by external sounds and unwanted thoughts. What can I do?

Keep practising by doing a little bit each day. If you have a spare five minutes when you are alone, just do a mini session. You will probably find it gradually gets easier and you will be able to extend your period of concentration.

I find it really hard to visualise things at all, but I would like to use the method to work on dream re-entry. What can I do?

Some people do not think in a very visual way and find the method difficult. You could try writing your dream down as a story and then adding to it and retelling bits of it until it feels right. Or you could draw or paint your dream.

CASE STUDIES

Jo saves Lucy from falling

Jo decides to re-enter the dream in which Lucy fell down the castle tower. She visualises Lucy just before she fell, swinging from the roof of the tower. Jo asks Lucy why she was doing this. Lucy says 'I'm showing you how clever I am. I'm a big girl now.' Jo understands that Lucy is beginning to want a bit of independence. She decides to spread a safety net under Lucy, rather than stop her climbing. When Lucy falls again she falls safely into this net. She thinks this is great fun and bounces about happily in it. Jo feels happy too, because the child is now safe.

Sarah sacks her new boss

Sarah dreams that she has a new job in an office. The office is dark and dingy and her new boss is harsh and over-bearing. Sarah decides to go back into this dream and put a few things right. When she goes back into her dream office she makes a large window with a view of the sea. Then she cleans it thoroughly and puts some plants here and there. When the horrid boss bounces in to see what is going on, she tells him that he is sacked! She is now in control of her own work environment and it feels much better.

James realises he doesn't want to arrive at work

James continues to have frustrating dreams about trying to get to work on time and encountering all manner of obstacles. He decides to go back into one of these dreams and put everything right. This time his shoes match, the front door is not jammed and the train is on time. He arrives at work with ten minutes in hand, feeling relaxed and in control. But as he opens the door to his office, the true meaning of his delay dreams strikes him. He doesn't want to go inside – he doesn't actually want to arrive at work at all. He knows now that his dreams are encouraging him to make a big change.

CHECKLIST

1. Practise creative visualisation whenever you can, even if it is only for a few minutes at a time.

2. Learn how to work on your dreams by re-entering them and altering things that are not right for you.

3. If you have a problem, try using the instant symbol method to help you to arrive at a solution.

4. Begin to work with protectors and guardians who will help you in the dream world.

5. Find your place of peace and visit it often.

10
Working with Other People

RUNNING A DREAM GROUP

Starting your group

When you have become more confident with working on your own dreams, you may like to consider working with other people in a small group. If there does not seem to be a suitable group running in your area, then you could consider starting your own group.

You could begin by sharing your dreams with other members of your own family. This can help partners and children to express their feelings more openly. If this idea does not seem right, then perhaps you have a few good friends who would be interested in starting up a dream group. You could consider advertising your group, but bear in mind that this means you may be working with total strangers.

A dream group might form naturally as you begin to discuss your dreams with other people and gradually discover that you have a mutual interest. There are quite a few advantages of working together on your dreams, instead of simply working alone all the time:

- Sharing a dream can make the dream more significant.

- People in the group can offer one another mutual support and acceptance.

- You can gain new insights into your dreams when you do group work. These come partly from feedback from the other members of the group, and partly from the impact of speaking your dream aloud.

- It is fun sharing dreams and relating within the group.

Your dream group doesn't need to be formal in its approach. In fact you may like to combine the dream work with other shared activities, such as having a meal together. Each member could bring his or her own contribution of food or drink for the evening. This works well – nobody has all the work to do and it gives the occasion a feeling of enjoyable fun and sociability. Each person needs to bring his or her dream diary along as well.

Discussing what you want from your group

When you decide to set up your dream group, there are a few points to consider at the first meeting:

- Begin by letting the individuals talk about themselves for a few minutes as a form of introduction. You don't need to go into great detail, just let the others know who you are and what are your main interests.

- Decide where you are going to hold your meetings. Usually a private house is the best place, and you may find that it is best to rotate houses, going to a different one each time. This means that the job of hosting the event is shared.

- How often do you want to meet? About once a fortnight is probably ideal, but this may not suit all members.

- Decide on the number of members you want. A small group of no more than half a dozen or so is best. This means that all the people get a chance to talk about their dreams, and members don't feel inhibited by revealing their innermost thoughts to a whole lot of people.

- Clarify the aims of the group by discussing what each person hopes to get out of meeting. This helps to get to know one another better.

- You might like to discuss having a small ceremony at the beginning of each meeting. This could be as simple as lighting a candle and sitting in silence for five minutes before you begin. A ceremony like this helps to set the atmosphere for the evening and calm everybody down a bit before you begin to share your dreams.

The idea of working in a group is not to interpret other people's dreams for them. If you do that, then as often as not you are just projecting your own ideas onto them, and usually barking up the wrong tree. Try instead to ask questions and offer suggestions. If a person feels that your suggestion is not right, then allow them to reject it. Similarly, don't feel that you necessarily have to take other people's ideas about your own dreams on board.

ACTING OUT YOUR DREAM

Using the whole group
The dream group setting gives you an opportunity to work with your dream further by acting it out. This can help bring a dream to life and see how characters can interact. Two or three members of the group are chosen to act the main characters. Usually the person whose dream it is takes the lead role. He or she can also be the director; or sometimes another person can be chosen to do this.

To begin with, read out the dream and then allow any comments to arise as to how the dream should be acted out. When the dream 'play' is underway, try to allow the characters free rein. The idea is not really to act out a strict version of the dream, so much as to allow the characters to develop in any way that seems appropriate. Acting out a dream is more like a dream re-entry.

- You can alter the story line or the script as you go along.

- A different ending can be allowed to emerge if it seems helpful to the dreamer.

- The characters can feel free to express whatever emotions they wish. This is especially valuable for dreams involving fear or anger.

- Other group members can supply support and encouragement. For example they could supply a cushion to beat up if a person expresses rage, or stand by to comfort people who get upset.

Acting out dreams in this way can be very valuable because people feel supported by the rest of the group and feel that their emotions are being validated.

Acting your dream solo
Another variation of acting out your dream is where the dreamer chooses to act out all the roles. This works best with dreams where there are only two main characters. A chair or cushion is placed to represent the position of the two characters. The dreamer then acts out the two characters in turn, physically moving position whenever the other character speaks.

This method is very good for dreams where you want to get a new angle on the viewpoint of a character in your dream. For example, supposing you are being pursued by a monster in your dream. Try asking the monster why it is pursuing you. Then swap chairs or

Fig. 11. The dragon – monster or guardian?

cushions, and actually be the monster. Allow the monster to have its say, then swap back into your own role and so on.

TALKING TO DREAM FIGURES

During sessions of acting out a dream you will probably find that interesting dialogues develop between the characters. The dialogue need not necessarily have occurred at all in the original dream. You can take this a step further and imagine that you actually meet a dream character and then hold a conversation with that character. This can be useful for developing dreams that feel especially important or revelatory to the dreamer. It is also good for working with nightmares, such as Sarah's 'tall flobbery monster' dream. Dialogues develop best when the dream group members know one another well and feel safe within the group setting.

Developing a dialogue
If a character keeps persistently turning up in your dreams then it can be a good idea to develop a dialogue of this sort. The dreamer becomes the character, and other members of the group pose questions to him or her. Sometimes it is not clear why a character is appearing in your dreams until you actually become that character. Then the words seem to take over and the character comes alive. Remember that you can see each character in your dream as an aspect of yourself, or as an aspect of an important relationship or problem in your life.

With a little practice you can become very imaginative and hold conversations not only with human characters, but also with animals and even inanimate objects from a dream. For example, Jo kept dreaming about a table, so she decided to hold a conversation with it.

Group member 'Who are you?'

Jo 'I am a table.'

Group member 'Why do you keep appearing in Jo's dreams?'

Jo 'Because I'm flat. People keep putting things on me. They just load more and more onto me until you can't see my original surface at all.'

Jo realised when she said this that she did feel rather flat at the moment. She felt put upon and and that her true self was being submerged by the demands of others.

DRAWING YOUR DREAM

It can be interesting to include sessions of drawing and painting in
your dream group's work together. Each person can choose a dream,
not necessarily their own, that they would like to work with. You can
either try to depict a whole scene from the dream, or else you can
choose one particular aspect, such as a symbol, a colour, an animal, a
monster and so on. You don't need to be a great artist, so don't worry
about the way the picture looks. The point is to try and express ideas
in a new way. Your group may like to try out some of the following
ideas:

- Make a picture of a nightmare, or a horrifying image from a dream.

- Try illustrating a recurring dream. Which aspects emerge as being
  the most important ones in the picture?

- Try to recall a childhood dream and then do a picture of it.

- Use a large sheet of paper and divide it in half. On one half
  illustrate an unhappy dream. Then, on the other half of the paper
  draw the same dream but this time with a happy ending.

- Each person in the group closes their eyes, asks for an instant
  symbol; and then does a picture of their symbol. Can you find any
  connections between the images produced by your group?

- Do a detailed picture of a dream house or a house that you visualise
  in your mind.

- Get the whole group to relax and visualise a special place of peace.
  Then either create individual pictures, or else work on a large group
  picture which incorporates everyone's ideas.

- Create pictures of your inner child when he or she is happy, sad and
  angry.

- Try illustrating a favourite fairy story or myth. You could just
  choose one special aspect of the story if you wish, such as a dragon
  or a magical sword.

- Make a mandala. This is a personal power symbol, usually round
  in shape. Choose symbols and colours from your dreams
  that have empowered you. You can add to your mandala
  gradually, building it up until it really means something to you
  personally.

CREATIVE WRITING ON A DREAM THEME

This is another idea for exploring dreams that works well in a group setting. You can write a story based on one of your own dreams, or you can use someone else's idea. Your group may like to try some of the following, and then explore further ideas of your own:

- Write a story based on your worst nightmare. Add to it and embellish it as you wish.

- Describe a nasty dream monster in as much detail as you can.

- Write about meeting your inner child. Describe the setting where you meet as well.

- Choose an interesting dream character and then write a short story involving that character.

- Write a detailed description of a dream house. What alterations and home improvements would you like to make?

- Think about means of transport that you have come across in dreams and then write about some of them. Which ones appeal to you the most and why?

As with acting and drawing your dream, you don't need to be restricted by sticking to the original dream. Use the dream as a starting point and then allow your imagination to run riot.

Story-telling

Another variation upon creative writing is to have a story-telling session. One person starts the ball rolling with an idea from a dream, and then the next person takes up the theme and carries on with the story. This can carry on for as long as you wish and it can get quite hilarious.

CASE STUDIES

James joins a dream work group

When James describes an interesting dream of his to a friend at work, it turns out that she is also interested in dreams. She suggests that he try joining her dream work group, which meets once a month. James is uncertain at first about sharing his dreams publicly, but he decides to give it a try. He discovers that the people in the group are friendly and supportive, and soon begins to get fresh insights into his dreams. Once he gets to know the people better he feels more able to open up and discuss most of his dreams.

Jo's family join in with dream work

Jo finds that as she begins to discuss her dreams with the family, her children become interested too. Dreams soon become a regular topic of conversation at the breakfast table. Jo finds that this helps her to understand when something is bothering one of the children. She is quite surprised when Peter eventually begins to join in too. They begin to talk about dreams when they are lying in bed before going to sleep. This opens up discussions about problems in their marriage and at work.

Sarah forms a new dream work group

Sarah mentions her interest in dreams to four friends and between them they decide to form a dream work group. They agree to meet every other Wednesday at one another's houses. Meanwhile Sarah explains to her friends how to keep a dream diary. The group decide that it would be fun to share a meal before going on to do their dream work. The hostess of the week provides the main course and the others bring drinks, salad, pudding and chocolate. The group soon feel that they are gaining a lot of mutual support and look forward to their evenings together.

ACTIVITIES

1. Hold a brainstorming session to see what new ideas your group can think of for team work.

2. When the group has become well established, write down 'anonymously' the outline of dreams you might find it hard to talk about openly. Pool the pieces of paper, get each person to pick one out at random and discuss common areas of difficulty. Maintain respect for each others' anonymity.

3. Get the group to consider:
    – The most valuable aspects of working in a group.
    – To what extent group members' dreams reflect their different personalities.

CHECKLIST

1. If you decide that you would like to join a dream group, check your local paper or library to see if you can find one. If not, then why not consider starting your own?

2. Make the sessions in your dream work group enjoyable and relaxing. Never force your interpretations on another person.

3. Keep your group open to new suggestions.

4. Remember to keep your dream diary and dream dictionary up to date.

A Short Dream Dictionary

Accident. A message that you need to slow down and take more care of yourself.

Aeroplane. Looking at things from a higher view-point. Going up in the world.

Angel. This may be a special dream messenger, so listen carefully. Angels represent higher, spiritual ideas. Your angel may be a guardian angel who takes care of you.

Animal. Listen to your instinctive feelings. Take note of the type of animal as well. (See Chapter 6.)

Attic. The highest part of the house may represent your spiritual self. Also look and see what is *in* your attic. You may find things which you have stored away from the past and now need to be looked at again.

Baby. A new beginning. An idea, or insight. Is your baby contented or are you neglecting it or refusing responsibility for it? It may also represent your own 'inner baby' – the part of you that longs to be pampered and totally secure.

Baggage. Stuff that you are lugging about that you probably don't need any more. Resentments.

Basement. The hidden part of the psyche where you store stuff that you are afraid of. The root of your problem.

Bed. Security and warmth. Escaping from the real world. Sexual issues.

Bell. Can be a joyful omen or a warning. Look at the context in your dream.

Bird. Freedom. Joyful song. Take note of the type of bird.

Blood. Life force. Anger and fear. Menstrual blood represents power, fertility and release.

Boat. Water in dreams usually represents our emotions and the boat shows how we are coping with them. Is it a peaceful journey, or are you sailing on rough, frightening water?

Book. A lesson is being offered to you. What is the book about?

Bottle. You may be bottling something up. What does your bottle have in it? Is the lid on or off? What colour is the bottle?

Cage. Feeling trapped. Fear – are you making the cage yourself? Are you in it, or does it contain a fierce animal, or another person?

Car. A means of moving on. Is the car under your control? It may represent your physical self.

Cards. Fate – what sort of hand you are being dealt. Divining the future.

Cave. The hidden, unconscious inner self. A very primitive, archetypal dream symbol. Initiation. Sanctuary.

Child. Your own inner child self. The dream may be about something that brings back feelings from childhood, such as fear, helplessness, or uninhibited joy.

Church. Authority. Religious ideas. Faith, security, sanctuary. Depends a lot on your own views on religion.

Climbing. Working upwards towards a goal. Is it hard work or easy going? If you are climbing downwards you are probably beginning to explore your unconscious mind.

Clothes. The persona – the self that you present to the outside world. If they are outlandish then you may want to express yourself more. If too tight, you are growing out of your present image. Or maybe you just need to go on a diet!

Crying. Expressing emotions that you are not letting go of in your waking world. You need to pay attention to what this dream is saying.

Crystal. Clarity and purity. Also depends on the type of crystal or stone. (See Chapter 2.)

Dancing. Feeling happy and uninhibited.

Dawn. A new beginning. Something is dawning on you.

Death. A complete change. Releasing and letting go of the past. May also be a warning about your health, or that of another. Who is dying? What energies or type of situation does that person represent to you?

Devil. Fear. Somebody who manipulates you. Lust and earthly joys. May represent a part of yourself that you see as 'bad'.

Door. A way through. A transition. If it is open then you are ready for new discoveries.

Earthquake. An upheaval, especially an emotional one. Fear of changes which you see approaching.

Explosion. Sudden personal crisis. Usually to do with a relationship.

Falling. Loss of control. Falling down on the job. Partly depends if you are simply falling over, or falling into something or down something.

Fire. A dangerous situation, especially an emotional one. Sexual energy. Spiritual energy. Enthusiasm.

Flood. Overwhelming emotions.

Flowers. Messages of happiness and grace.

Flying. Astral travelling. Rising above your everyday world onto a more spiritual level.

Fog. Uncertainty and confusion.

Food. Can represent any kind of nourishment: physical, emotional, spiritual. Depends also on the kind of food, *eg* sweets for the sweet things in life, sausages are phallic *etc*.

Garden. Your place of peace. Doing something creative. Look at the plants in your garden: is it full of lovely flowers, or are there lots of weeds to be sorted out?

Gate. A way through, perhaps to another world, or to a new phase of your life. New opportunity.

Hair. Often comes into dreams if you are concerned about your physical self especially if your hair seems to be falling out (quite a common dream). Combing hair – getting rid of tangles in your life. Healthy hair – good health.

Hotel. A transition in your life, a temporary situation. Feeling unsettled.

House. Often represents the self. A large rambling house can mean that you are beginning to explore your own psyche. The house can be your physical or spiritual self. If there is something wrong with the house, look for a connection with what may be wrong with yourself *eg* the roof blowing off could be a situation in which you feel very exposed and vulnerable. (See Chapter 5.)

Island. Feeling isolated. Self-contained. A place of refuge.

Journey. Personal growth. If your journey is delayed, look at ways in which your progress is being blocked. The means of transport is also important, so are the people who are going with you, if any. (See Chapter 5.)

Judge. Your own alter-ego, that is the part of yourself that judges your own actions. Your inner parent. Make sure that you are not being over-critical of yourself

Key. The way forward, the means of opening a door. This may be on a physical or a spiritual level.

Killing. Something in your life that you need to get rid of. Maybe old behaviour or beliefs that are no longer appropriate. If it is a murder, then the situation probably involves anger. You may find that you are killing an animal, if so, what sort is it? If you are killing a child, this probably represents some childish behaviour.

Mine. A hidden source of treasure or strength. Going down deep into the subconscious.

Mirror. The mirror is showing you some aspect of yourself or your behaviour which you need to face.

Money. May show that you are worried about money. Richness of experience. Profitable actions. Energy.

Monster. Something that you are afraid of. You may need to confront this monster – they are often not as bad as they seem.

Moon. A powerful symbol of feminine psychic energy. Tides and rhythms, going with the flow, menstruation. New moon – new beginnings. Full moon – power and completion, fertility. Waning moon – getting rid of unwanted emotions.

Music. A beautiful dream symbol which may mean getting in touch with powerful spiritual forces. If the music is not harmonious however, then you are out of tune with something.

Nest. Safety and cosiness. Family and home. Incubating ideas.

Net. Trying to catch something – an idea perhaps? Or perhaps you feel trapped, unable to escape.

Path. Your life's path, the way to go. Look to see if the way is easy, or is it uphill, or overgrown?

Policeman. An authority figure. Guilt. What are you doing that you see as bad? Alternatively it may be a sign of care and protection.

Postman. Messages coming into your life. What sort of news does he bring?

Race. The rat race. Are you trying too hard to compete? Winning a race may represent a personal victory of some sort.

Rainbow. A symbol of faith and joy. A promise of better times ahead. Often appears after a period of emotional problems.

Ring. Marriage, promises, completion, love.

Rock. Safe place, strength. Or alternatively, being dashed against the rocks. An obstacle of some sort.

Roof. Feeling of security and safety. The roof is the top of the house, so it may show you the condition of your spiritual self.

Running. Depends partly if you are running **away** from something that you fear, or **towards** something exciting. If you are running away, try to stop and face the truth. Running fast may indicate an acceleration in your spiritual growth.

School. Lessons to be learnt, or a situation that reminds you of your childhood.

Seasons. Spring – new beginnings. Summer – fertility, growth, strength. Autumn – harvesting, letting go. Winter – resting, waiting, end of a cycle.

Stairs. Going up – success, rise in confidence, going up to more spiritual levels. Going down – loss of confidence, or exploring the subconscious.

Star. Hope and guidance. Something to look forward to. Higher beings who are showing you the way.

Sun. Joy and success. Confidence. Strength. Situation improving after a difficult time.

Sword. Attack or defence. Finding the truth of a situation.

Teeth. Often shows concern about your physical body. Wanting to attack or bite somebody. Teeth falling out – physical illness, or a transition time, such as that you went through as a child when your teeth really fell out.

Telephone. Messages and communication. Are you answering it?

Toilets. Getting rid of stuff you no longer need. May also be connected with deep-seated guilt or anxiety.

Trees. Your own development. Family matters. Is your tree small or large, straight or crooked? Has it got leaves on at the moment?

Uniform. Authority. Conforming. Are you being too rigid in some way? Or do you feel this about somebody else?

War. Anxiety and anger that is inside you and liable to erupt. Conflict.

Washing. Cleansing something, letting go.

Water. Emotional matters. Look at the type of water, where it is, what condition it is in, how deep it is and so on. (See Chapter 5.)

Waterfall. Emotional release. Healing.

Web. Feeling trapped or caught. Are you weaving it yourself? A complex situation.

Wheel. Life's ups and downs. Luck, good fortune. Travel.

Window. Looking at a situation in a different way. Looking at the future or the past. Seeking alternatives.

Glossary

Affirmation. An empowering statement used to encourage a positive state of mind.

Archetype. A mental image or pattern of thinking that is common to all human beings.

Astral body. Ethereal counterpart of the body supposed to travel far afield in dreams and to survive after death.

Coincidence. Events or circumstances that appear to be significantly connected, but not in a causal way.

Collective unconscious. The part of the unconscious concerned with ancestral memories and experiences common to all mankind.

Conscious. Awake and aware of one's identity and surroundings.

Creativity. The ability to be imaginative and inventive.

Dream-catcher. A decorative net hung above the bed to encourage dream recall.

Dream guide. An imaginary mentor, usually human or animal, who appears in your dreams and visualisations and helps you to work with them.

Dream stone. A special stone or crystal that helps you to incubate dreams and work on particular problems.

Essential oil. Volatile oil derived from a plant and used in aromatherapy.

Free association. A method of exploring spontaneous ideas arising from a given word or symbol.

Imagery. Pictures seen with the mind's eye.

Inner child. The part of the psyche that is still child-like.

Lucid dream. A dream during which one becomes aware that one is dreaming.

Mandala. Symbolic circular figure, representing the self's search for wholeness. In various religions it represents the universe.

Myth. A traditional story which tries to explain natural, social or religious phenomena.

Precognitive. Knowing beforehand, often by apparently supernatural means.

Projection. Attributing traits or actions to other people, as a defence against recognising them in oneself.

REM sleep. Cyclical periods of brain activity which occur during sleep and are associated with rapid eye movements.

Psyche. The whole of a person's inner, mental world.

Shadow. The part of the personality that is hidden from the conscious self.

Subconscious. The part of the mind that is not fully aware, but still influences our thoughts and actions.

Symbol. A thing that represents, typifies or recalls another thing.

Totem animal. An animal which represents and empowers an individual or a group of people.

Visualisation. The experiencing of visual imagery.

Further Reading

The Comprehensive Book of Dreams, Edwin Raphael (Foulsham, 1992).

Dream Dictionary, Tony Crisp (MacDonald, 1990).

The Dreaming Brain, Allan Hobson (Penguin, 1990).

Dream Interpretation for Beginners, Michele Simmons and Chris McLaughlin (Headway, 1994).

The Dream Pack, David Fontana (Reader's Digest).

Dream Power, Ann Faraday (Hodder and Stoughton, 1972).

Dream Spells, Claire Nahmad (Pavilion, 1994).

The Interpretation of Dreams, Sigmund Freud (new edn. Penguin, 1991).

Interpret Your Dreams – Unlock the Secrets of Your Unconscious, Pierre Daco (Robinson, 1995).

Man and His Symbols, Carl Jung (new edn. Pan Books, 1978).

The Mystic Dreambook – 2500 dreams explained (Foulsham, 1995).

Pocketful of Dreams, Denise Linn (Piatkus, 1993).

10,000 Dreams and Their Traditional Meanings (Foulsham, 1995).